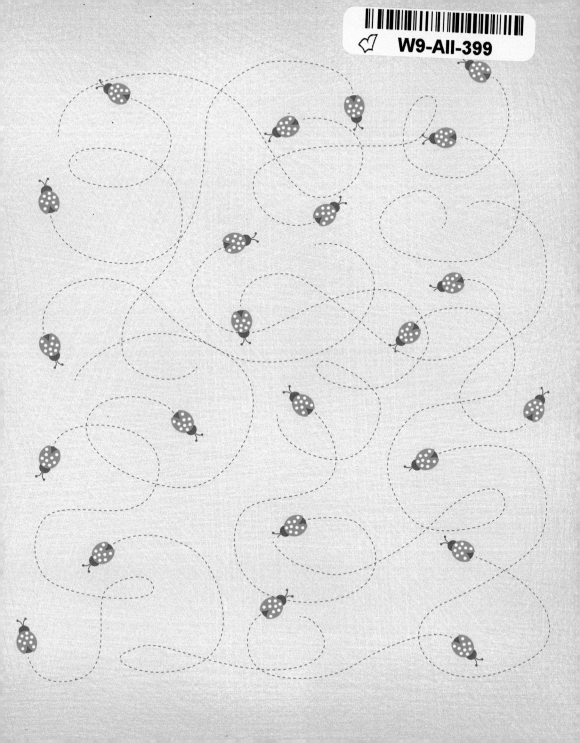

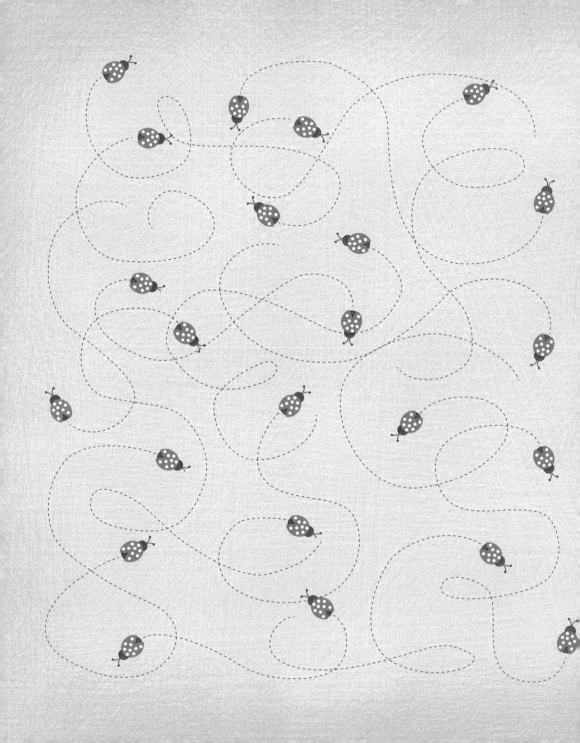

This book belongs to

_____

Given by

_____

The One Year®

my princess
devotions
preschool edition

Karen
Whiting

TYNDALE KIDS

Tyndale House Publishers, Inc.

Carol Stream, Illinois

Visit Tyndale's website for kids at www.tyndale.com/kids.

TYNDALE, The One Year, and One Year are registered trademarks of Tyndale House Publishers, Inc. The One Year logo and the Tyndale Kids logo are trademarks of Tyndale House Publishers, Inc.

The One Year My Princess Devotions: Preschool Edition

Designed by Jacqueline L. Nuñez

Edited by Erin Gwynne

Published in association with the Books & Such Literary Agency, Mary Keeley, 52 Mission Circle, Suite 122, PMB 170, Santa Rosa, CA 95409-5370.

For manufacturing information regarding this product, please call 1-800-323-9400.

ISBN 978-1-4143-6905-1

Printed in the United States of America

19   18   17   16   15   14   13
7   6   5   4   3   2   1

Dear Parents,

Most girls are enthralled with princess stories. They envision a princess as being loved, cherished, and surrounded by beauty. The good news is that every girl is a princess to God, the King of the universe. He loves each precious girl and surrounds her with the beautiful world he created.

   The daily moments with God in The One Year My Princess Devotions: Preschool Edition *help girls do more than understand that they are beloved princesses. Girls will learn about God the King and develop a sense of belonging to God's family as they apply his Word daily and become princesses in action.*

   Help your daughter start a great lifetime habit by making devotions a special part of her day. Devotions help nurture a relationship with God, and doing them together builds a child-parent bond. These devotions are perfect for morning or afternoon when girls can complete the simple actions that apply what they've learned from God's Word. You can count on God to be with you and your daughter as you spend time with him.

Karen Whiting

January

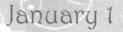

God Made Me Special!

Royal Words

How you [Lord] made me is amazing and wonderful. I praise you for that. What you have done is wonderful. I know that very well.

Psalm 139:14

Princess Thoughts

Wow! God made you special! He chose to make your hair curly or straight. He picked the color of your eyes and the color of your skin. He chose the shape of your nose. He even chose how tall you will grow!

A Prayer for the King

Dear Father God, thank you for making me special and choosing my eyes, hair, and skin.

Princess in Action

Look in a mirror and see how God chose to make you. What color are your eyes? Do you have curly or straight hair? What color is your hair? God loves how you look. Tell someone else today that God made him or her special too.

Made with Love

Royal Words

You [Lord] created the deepest parts of
my being. You put me together.

PSALM 139:13

Princess Thoughts

God made every single part of you, from your head to your
feet. He took time to make you just the way he wanted you to
look. And God loves how you look!

A Prayer for the King

God, thanks for taking time to make me, from the top of my
head to the tips of my toes.

Princess in Action

Put a puzzle together, one piece at a time. Look at the puzzle when
you have finished. It looks great! Talk with your mom or dad about
how God had fun putting you together. You look great!

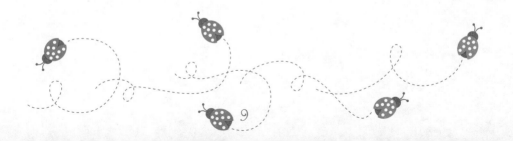

A Beautiful Smile

Royal Words

[God] will fill your mouth with laughter.
Shouts of joy will come from your lips.

JOB 8:21

Princess Thoughts

God made your mouth! He gave you pretty teeth and a wonderful
smile to make you beautiful on the outside.

A Prayer for the King

Father, thanks for my teeth and my pretty smile.

Princess in Action

Care for your teeth by brushing them after you eat.
Look at your princess smile in the mirror,
and be sure to smile at everyone you see.

Hair Fun

Royal Words

[Your heavenly Father] even counts
every hair on your head!
MATTHEW 10:30

Princess Thoughts

Try counting your hairs, and you'll see you have lots of hair!
You have about 100,000 hairs on your head. That's a lot!
Did you know that God has even numbered each one?
He knows you right down to the last hair on your head,
whether it is straight, curly, red, brown, black, or yellow.

A Prayer for the King

Thank you, Father, for caring about every inch of me,
including each and every hair!

Princess in Action

Take care of the hair God gave you. It's like a crown. Have
fun with a hair party. Do your mom's or sister's hair! Tell your
mom or sister, "God loves you so much that he counts every
one of your hairs!"

God Has a Plan for You

Royal Words

"I know the plans I have for you," announces the Lord. "I want you to enjoy success. I do not plan to harm you. I will give you hope for the years to come." JEREMIAH 29:11

Princess Thoughts

God cares about what you will do tomorrow and all the days to come. He made good plans for you. He may have given you legs that can run fast, feet that can kick a soccer ball far, or hands that can draw pretty pictures. Follow God's ways, and practice the things you are good at doing. Then you'll be ready to do all that God has planned for you.

A Prayer for the King

Thank you, Father, for making plans for my great future. Show me what you want me to do each day.

Princess in Action

Look at a calendar and see all the days in this year. On today's date have someone write in one thing you're good at (this is called a talent). Draw a crown on the date. Try to use your talent as often as you can. Look for ways to use it to help others.

January 6

Growing Up

Royal Words

The boys grew up. Esau became a skillful hunter. He
was a man who liked the open country. But Jacob was
a quiet man. He stayed at home among the tents.

GENESIS 25:27

Princess Thoughts

Twin brothers, Esau and Jacob, grew up. One was noisy and liked
to work outside. The other was quiet and liked to work inside.
We may like different things, but we are all special to God.

A Prayer for the King

Thank you, Father, for making me special and different from
everyone else.

Princess in Action

You have favorite things you like to do. Talk about some of them.
Maybe you like to sing, color, or play ball. Use what you like to do
to help someone. If you like to sing, sing a song to someone. If you
like to play ball, teach someone how to play a game with a ball.

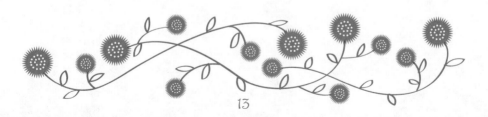

January 7

Listen and Do God's Word

Royal Words

Don't just listen to the word. You fool yourselves
if you do that. You must do what it says.

JAMES 1:22

Princess Thoughts

God wants us to listen to him. He also wants us to do
what he tells us to do. As you do what God's Word says
to do, you will be following God's plan for you.

A Prayer for the King

Lord, help me to be a doer of your Word.

Princess in Action

Learn God's words by heart so you can do them.
Start by memorizing the verse you read in today's
Royal Words section.

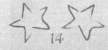

A New Person

Royal Words
Anyone who believes in Christ is a new creation.
The old is gone! The new has come!
2 CORINTHIANS 5:17

Princess Thoughts
When we love and obey Jesus, we act more like him.
That makes us new!

A Prayer for the King
Thank you, Father, for making me new on the inside.

Princess in Action
Dress up like a princess in God's family. Have someone
take a photo of you. The next time you feel upset and
want to whine, look at that picture. Remember that
Jesus wants you to be nice.

I Can Care for a Baby

Royal Words

Shiphrah and Puah had respect for God. So he
gave them families of their own.

Exodus 1:21

Princess Thoughts

Shiphrah and Puah helped other women in Bible times have
babies, just like doctors and nurses help today. The mean pharaoh
wanted Shiphrah and Puah to hurt the Hebrew baby boys.
These women didn't obey Pharaoh, though, because they believed
in God. God gave them their own babies to love.

A Prayer for the King

Thank you, Father, for the doctors and nurses who helped
my mommy have me! Help me to always remember that
babies are special.

Princess in Action

Practice taking care of a baby with your doll. Put on her clothes,
hold her, and rock her.

January 10

A Beautiful Baby

Royal Words
[Jochebed] became pregnant and had a son by [her
husband]. She saw that her baby [Moses] was a
fine child. So she hid him for three months.
EXODUS 2:2

Princess Thoughts
Jochebed had a beautiful baby boy named Moses. She loved
Moses very much. But mean people wanted to hurt all of the
Hebrew baby boys. So Jochebed hid baby Moses in a basket
to keep him safe.

A Prayer for the King
Thank you, Father, for giving me a mother who loves
me, keeps me safe, and sees my beauty.

Princess in Action
Look at your baby pictures. Ask your mom how she felt when
she first saw you, her little princess. Make a card for your
mom to let her know how much you love her.

I Love My Mommy

Royal Words
Adam and Eve had a son. Then Eve said, "I'll name him Cain because I got him with the help of the LORD."
GENESIS 4:1, CEV

Princess Thoughts
Eve was the first mother on earth. She understood that God made the baby in her belly. Eve felt her baby, Cain, wiggle, kick, and roll. God chose your mother for you. Mothers are so special! They love their babies very much.

A Prayer for the King
Father God, thank you for my mother who loves me and takes care of me.

Princess in Action
Hug your mother. Thank God for making her! Your mother is a princess too. Make paper crowns. Take pictures wearing your crowns.

My Daddy

Royal Words

[The son] got up and went to his father. While the
son was still a long way off, his father saw him. He
was filled with tender love for his son. He ran to him.
He threw his arms around him and kissed him.

LUKE 15:20

Princess Thoughts

A son ran away from home. He didn't want to follow rules.
He wanted to do whatever he felt like doing. But he ran out of
food and money. Grr. His stomach growled. He felt so hungry!
He wanted to say, "Dad, I'm sorry." He ran home. His dad saw him
and ran to him. His dad hugged and kissed him. His dad was
happy that his son had come home.

A Prayer for the King

Thank you, God, for giving me a father. Help me to obey my dad.

Princess in Action

Do what your father asks you to do. Give your father a big hug!
Draw a picture for your dad. Pray for your dad.

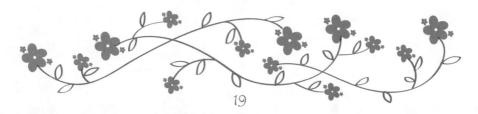

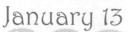

A Baby Is Named

Royal Words

Abraham gave the name Isaac to the son Sarah had by
him. . . . Sarah said, "God has given laughter to me.
Everyone who hears about this will laugh with me."

GENESIS 21:3, 6

Princess Thoughts

The name Isaac means "laughter." Isaac's mother and father felt
very happy to have a child. They had waited a long time for Isaac,
so they gave him a name to show their joy. Your parents chose
your name. God wants you to bring laughter to your parents too.

A Prayer for the King

Thank you, Father, for my name. Help me to bring
laughter to my parents.

Princess in Action

Try to make your parents laugh by making funny faces.
Ask your parents why they chose your name.

I Can Obey

Royal Words

Children, obey your parents in everything.
That pleases the Lord.
COLOSSIANS 3:20

Princess Thoughts

One way to make God smile is to obey your mommy and daddy.
Do what they tell you to do right away. And do it with a smile,
because that pleases your parents and God!

A Prayer for the King

God, please help me to obey my parents today.

Princess in Action

Listen to your parents today and do what your mommy
and daddy tell you to do.

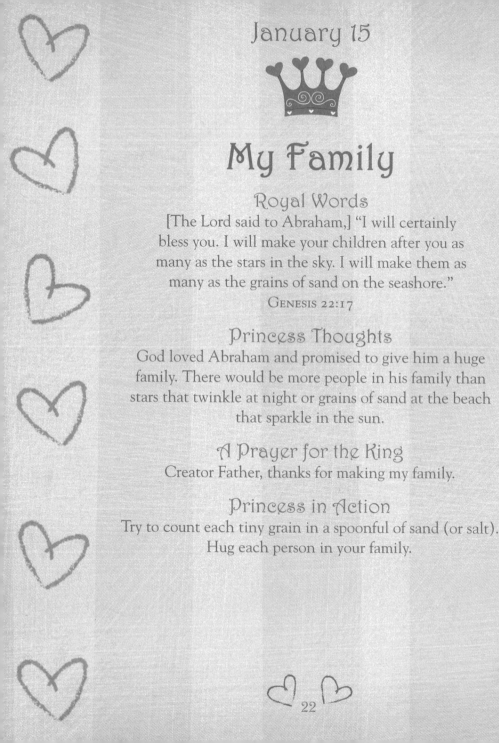

My Family

Royal Words

[The Lord said to Abraham,] "I will certainly bless you. I will make your children after you as many as the stars in the sky. I will make them as many as the grains of sand on the seashore."

GENESIS 22:17

Princess Thoughts

God loved Abraham and promised to give him a huge family. There would be more people in his family than stars that twinkle at night or grains of sand at the beach that sparkle in the sun.

A Prayer for the King

Creator Father, thanks for making my family.

Princess in Action

Try to count each tiny grain in a spoonful of sand (or salt). Hug each person in your family.

God's Family

Royal Words

Some people did accept him [Jesus]. They believed in his name. He gave them the right to become children of God.

JOHN 1:12

Princess Thoughts

God wants you to be his child. He wants you and all of your family to be part of his big family that will live in heaven with him forever! All you have to do is believe that Jesus died on the cross for your sins and ask him to forgive you for the bad things you've done.

A Prayer for the King

God, thank you for asking me to be a part of your family.

Princess in Action

If you want to be a part of God's family, talk to your mom or dad about it. Then you can pray and tell God that you want to join his family.

Loving People

Royal Words

[Jesus said,] "If you love one another, everyone
will know you are my disciples."
JOHN 13:35

Princess Thoughts

God wants us to love other people. This way they will see
that we follow Jesus and will want to follow him too.

A Prayer for the King

Lord, help me to love the people I see today.

Princess in Action

Show love by being a kind princess. Smile at everyone you see.
Make a crown for one of your friends.

January 18

My Creator God

Royal Words

At the beginning of creation, God "made them male and female."
MARK 10:6

Princess Thoughts

God made everyone on earth—every man, woman, girl,
and boy who ever lived! God made you. He's your King,
and you're his little princess!

A Prayer for the King

Dear Father, thank you for filling the earth with all kinds of people
who can laugh, talk, smile, and play.

Princess in Action

Take a people-watching walk with your mom or dad. Bundle
up if it's cold outside. As you walk, look at all the different
people God made. Think about how God made each person
special and loves everyone he made.

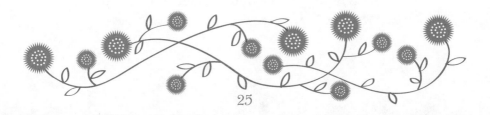

Being Helpful

Royal Words

After [Rebekah] had given him a drink, she said, "I'll get water for your camels too. I'll keep doing it until they finish drinking." So she quickly emptied her jar into the stone tub. Then she ran back to the well to get more water. She got enough for all of his camels.

GENESIS 24:19-20

Princess Thoughts

Rebekah gave a man a drink and noticed his camels looked thirsty. She offered to give them water. Camels drink lots of water, so she must have filled many buckets! The man had prayed that God would send someone who would give water to the camels. Rebekah was the answer to his prayers.

A Prayer for the King

Lord, thank you for water that tastes so good when I'm thirsty. Please help me to see how I can help animals when they're thirsty too.

Princess in Action

If you have a cat or dog, help your mom or dad get water for it. If you don't have a pet, put water outside for birds to drink.

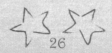

January 20

God's Creatures

Royal Words

The Lord God had formed all of the wild animals. He had also formed all of the birds of the air. He had made all of them out of the ground. He brought them to [Adam] to see what names he would give them. And the name the man gave each living creature became its name.

GENESIS 2:19

Princess Thoughts

God asked Adam to name all of the animals. Adam gave God's creatures names like chimpanzee, aardvark, and hippopotamus! God also asked Adam to care for everything God made. God, the King of Creation, wants his princesses to help take care of the animals too.

A Prayer for the King

Dear Father, thank you for making amazing creatures!

Princess in Action

A princess needs to care about everything made by God, the King. Talk with your mom or dad about ways you can take care of the animals around you.

God's Birds

Royal Words

Look at the birds of the air. They don't plant or gather crops. They don't put away crops in storerooms. But your Father who is in heaven feeds them. Aren't you worth much more than they are?

MATTHEW 6:26

Princess Thoughts

God cares for the birds. He cares for tiny sparrows and large eagles, as well as pink flamingos. God treasures you even more than birds. He will always take care of you.

A Prayer for the King

Thank you for filling the sky with birds that sing and flap their wings. Father, thanks for taking care of me, too.

Princess in Action

Go outside and watch the birds flying in the sky. Toss birdseed or dried fruit on the ground to help feed God's birds.

January 22

I Can Help Keep God's World Beautiful

Royal Words

The earth belongs to the Lord. And so does everything in it. The world belongs to him. And so do all those who live in it.

Psalm 24:1

Princess Thoughts

The world belongs to God because he made it! He made giant trees, little crawling bugs, twittering birds, and bright-colored flowers. You belong to God too. He wants everyone, especially his princesses, to keep the world he made beautiful.

A Prayer for the King

Thank you, God, for making such a wonderful world and filling it with so many different animals, plants, and people.

Princess in Action

Make a litter bag for your car. Add ribbon to the top of a paper or plastic bag to make a handle, and hang the bag over a headrest. This will help keep your car and God's world clean.

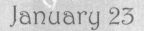

Tree Problems

Royal Words

He went to the man who took care of the vineyard. He said,
"For three years now I've been coming to look for fruit on this fig tree.
But I haven't found any. Cut it down! Why should it use up the soil?"
"Sir," the man replied, "leave it alone for one more year.
I'll dig around it and feed it. If it bears fruit next year, fine!
If not, then cut it down."

LUKE 13:7-9

Princess Thoughts

A tree needs food to help it grow and make fruit. It takes time for the
tree to grow. The gardener in the Bible story didn't want to chop the
tree down right away. He wanted to wait a little longer. The gardener
planned to take special care of the tree so it would bear fruit.

A Prayer for the King

Lord, thank you for fruit trees that make good food. Help us to be
patient in caring for trees and plants.

Princess in Action

Take a walk and look at the plants and trees
in your neighborhood.
Water one that looks thirsty.

God Hung the Sun, Moon, and Stars in the Sky

Royal Words

[The Lord] made the great lights in the sky. *His faithful love continues forever.* He made the sun to rule over the day. *His faithful love continues forever.* He made the moon and stars to rule over the night. *His faithful love continues forever.*

PSALM 136:7-9

Princess Thoughts

God made the sun that shines, the moon that glows, and the stars that sparkle. He hung them in the sky to give us light both day and night.

A Prayer for the King

Thank you, Lord, for creating sunlight, moonlight, and starlight.

Princess in Action

Look at the stars at night. If you can't see the stars in the sky, make your own stars. Ask your mom or dad to help you put holes in a piece of black paper. Shine a flashlight through it at night, and see the lights twinkle.

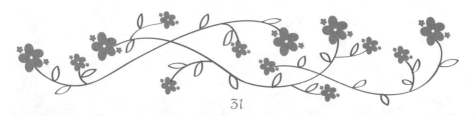

I Can Make God Smile

Royal Words

The LORD said to Noah, "Go into the ark with your whole family.
I know that you are a godly man among the people of today."

SENESIS 7:1

Princess Thoughts

One day a long time ago, God looked around the earth and found only
one good person. He found Noah. Noah made God smile! God planned
to send a lot of rain so that the earth would flood and all the bad people
would go away. God wanted to save Noah, Noah's family, and two of
every kind of animal. So God asked Noah to build a boat.

A Prayer for the King

Creator Father, help me to do good things that make you smile.

Princess in Action

When you help others, you make God smile. Help your mom
wash dishes in the sink today. Add the soap to make bubbles.
See how the water cleans the dishes. See if you can get a plate
so clean it squeaks when you push your finger across it.
That's a plate clean enough for a princess.

A Big Flood

Royal Words

The waters rose higher and higher on the earth.
And the ark floated on the water.

Genesis 7:18

Princess Thoughts

Long ago God covered the earth with water to get rid of all the bad people. He sent Noah and Noah's family and two of each animal into a big boat called an ark to save them. *Drip. Drop.* It rained and rained. Water filled the earth, but the boat floated on the water. Everyone on board the ark was safe.

A Prayer for the King

Thank you, God, for keeping me safe, just like you kept Noah and his family and the animals safe.

Princess in Action

Splish! Splash! Fill a bowl with water. Drop different objects in it to see what floats and what sinks. Whenever an item floats, thank God for one way he keeps you safe.

God's Promise to Me

Royal Words

[God said,] "I have put my rainbow in the clouds. It will be the sign of the covenant [promise] between me and the earth."

GENESIS 9:13

Princess Thoughts

After the Flood, God sent sunshine and dried up all the water. Then he filled the sky with a beautiful rainbow. God promised Noah he would never again flood the whole earth.

A Prayer for the King

Father God, thank you for the rainbow and for keeping your promise to never flood the earth again.

Princess in Action

Draw a rainbow on a paper plate. Add glitter to make the rainbow sparkle. Hang it on a wall in your room. Every time you see the rainbow, you can remember that God has kept his promise to never flood the earth again.

January 28

Being a Christian

Royal Words
At Antioch the believers were called Christians for the first time.
Acts 11:26

Princess Thoughts
People were first called Christians after Jesus rose from the
dead and went back to heaven. Now there are many
Christians. Jesus wants everyone to follow him and be a
Christian. He wants you to follow him too!

A Prayer for the King
Father King, thanks for sending Jesus.

Princess in Action
Make a thank-you card for Jesus. Decorate the card
with glitter for a princess sparkle. Tell someone
about Jesus today.

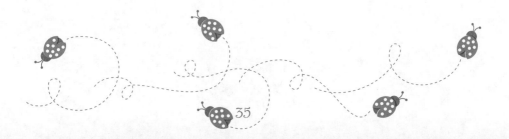

A Tiny Seed

Royal Words

[Jesus] replied, "Suppose you have faith as small as a mustard seed. Then you can say to this mulberry tree, 'Be pulled up. Be planted in the sea.' And it will obey you."

LUKE 17:6

Princess Thoughts

God made tall mountains and tiny seeds. He is so powerful, yet he tells us that our prayers can make a big difference. We just have to believe that he hears us. When we pray, we ask God to use his power to help us.

A Prayer for the King

Thank you, Father, for listening to my prayers.

Princess in Action

Have your mom or dad help you write prayers you want God to answer. Put them on your refrigerator, and pray every day. Draw a crown next to each prayer when God answers it. He loves you and wants to answer your prayers.

January 30

When Languages Began

Royal Words

The Lord mixed up the language of the whole world there. That's
why the city was named Babel. From there the Lord scattered
[the people] over the face of the whole earth.

GENESIS 11:9

Princess Thoughts

Have you heard someone speak words you don't understand? That
person is probably using a different language, like Spanish or French.
Once upon a time, everyone on the earth spoke the same language.
Then people tried to build a tower to heaven. They wanted to be bigger
than God. But God stopped the bad plan by making the people speak
different languages. They couldn't understand each other anymore!

A Prayer for the King

Father, I'm glad you understand my words, no matter which
language I speak.

Princess in Action

Look at a map of the world. Find out what languages are spoken
in different parts of the world. Pray for people in each country you
talk about. It doesn't matter which language you use. God always
listens to your princess prayers.

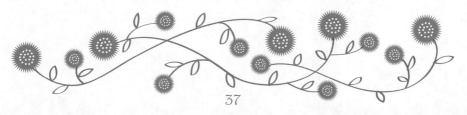

The Same in All Languages

Royal Words

Why, then, do we each hear them speaking
in our own native language?

Acts 2:8

Princess Thoughts

One special day people who spoke different languages
heard the words that the apostle Peter said and
understood what he was saying. They were amazed!
God's message is always the same in every language.
He loves us!

A Prayer for the King

Thank you, God, for loving all people. Help me
to share your love with others.

Princess in Action

Learn to say "Jesus loves you" in a few different
languages: *Jesus liebt dich* (German); *Jesús te ama*
(Spanish); *Jésus vous aime* (French); *Jesus älskar dig*
(Swedish); and *Jisu e lomani iko* (Fijian).

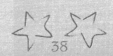

February

February 1

Agreeing with God

Royal Words

Obey me. Then I will be your God. And you will
be my people. Live the way I command you to
live. Then things will go well with you.

JEREMIAH 7:23

Princess Thoughts

God wants to be our God. He wants us to be part of his family.
God says that if we obey him, he will take care of us. This
agreement between God and those who obey him is called
a covenant. God always keeps his promises.

A Prayer for the King

Thank you, Father, for promising to take care of me.
Please help me to obey you.

Princess in Action

It's important to keep promises. Make a promise today.
Maybe you could promise to clean your room. Your
mommy or daddy could promise to read a special book or
play a game with you when you keep your promise.

February 2

A Place for God's Word

Royal Words

[Moses] got the tablets of the covenant. He placed them in the ark. He put the poles through its rings. And he put the cover on it.

EXODUS 40:20

Princess Thoughts

God wrote his rules on stone blocks, which are called tablets in the Bible. These ten rules are known as the Ten Commandments. Moses placed the tablets in a special place. Today the Bible tells us about God and his rules. We need to take care of the Bible because the Bible has God's words in it.

A Prayer for the King

Thank you, Father, for giving me the Bible to learn about you. Help me to remember to take care of it.

Princess in Action

If you have a Bible, think of a special place you can put it. Be gentle when turning the pages. Be careful when you put it away.

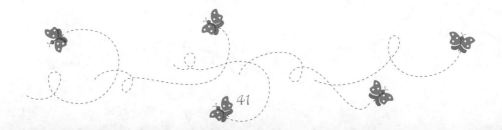

Night-Lights

Royal Words

The rules of the LORD are right. They give joy
to our hearts. The commands of the LORD shine
brightly. They give light to our minds.

PSALM 19:8

Princess Thoughts

When it's dark outside, lights help us to see where we're
going so we can know where to walk safely and not trip.
God's rules in the Bible show us how to behave. If we
obey his rules, we will be happy.

A Prayer for the King

Thank you, Lord, for giving me the Bible to help me
make the right choices.

Princess in Action

Plug in a night-light in your room. Then turn off the
lights. When you look at the night-light, remember
to thank God for giving you the Bible that guides you
to make good choices.

February 4

Follow the Leader

Royal Words
Your throne, O God, will last for ever and ever; a scepter
of justice will be the scepter of your kingdom.
HEBREWS 1:8, NIV

Princess Thoughts
Did you know that God is the leader of a kingdom? He holds a
scepter and sits on his throne in heaven, just like some of the
kings in the Bible did. A scepter looks like a wand. It is a sign that
the king is in charge. It is also like a staff a shepherd uses to guide
his sheep. God is a leader who guides us.

A Prayer for the King
Thank you, God, for being a leader who shows us
what to do and where to go.

Princess in Action
Make a scepter from cardboard or a paper towel roll.
Play Follow the Leader, taking turns holding the scepter
and showing each other what to do.

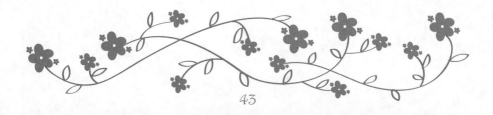

Follow the Light of Jesus

Royal Words

[Jesus] said, "I am the light of the world. Those
who follow me will never walk in darkness.
They will have the light that leads to life."

JOHN 8:12

Princess Thoughts

Sometimes it's scary to be in the dark. But if someone
turns on the light, we can see what's around us. We don't
have to be afraid about anything, because Jesus promises
to always be with us. He is the Light of the World.

A Prayer for the King

Thank you, Jesus, for being my light.

Princess in Action

Turn out the lights and let your mom or dad shine a
flashlight. Run to where the light shines. Talk about
how Jesus wants to light your way.

Traffic Lights and Rules

Royal Words

Be very strong. Be careful to obey everything that is written in the Scroll of the Law of Moses. Don't turn away from it to the right or the left.

Joshua 23:6

Princess Thoughts

God told the people to obey him and not turn away from him. He also told them to be strong. God didn't mean that people need strong muscles. He meant that they need to always make good choices, even when it's easier to disobey.

A Prayer for the King

Lord, help me to be strong and to always obey you.

Princess in Action

Obeying God keeps you safe like obeying traffic lights keeps people safe when driving. Watch the traffic-light colors when you're in the car.
Red means stop. Green means go.
Yellow means slow down.

God's First Big Rule

Royal Words

Jesus replied, "Love the Lord your God with all your heart and with all your soul. Love him with all your mind."

MATTHEW 22:37

Princess Thoughts

A man asked Jesus what was the most important of God's rules. Jesus answered that the most important rule is to love God. If we love God, we will want to do what makes him happy, and that will help us follow all of his other rules.

A Prayer for the King

Lord, help me to love you with all my heart, soul, and mind.

Princess in Action

Blow kisses to God. Before each kiss, say something great about God like, "God, you are so wonderful." This is a way to show God that you love him.

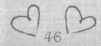

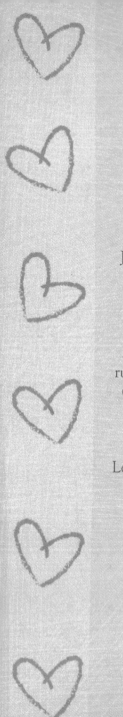

February 8

God's Second Big Rule

Royal Words

The second [commandment] is like [the first].
"Love your neighbor as you love yourself."

MATTHEW 22:39

Princess Thoughts

Jesus told people that the second most important rule for
us to follow is also about love. God wants us to love our
neighbor just as much as we love ourselves. He wants us
to be nice to them and to pray for them.

A Prayer for the King

Lord, help me to love all the people around me.

Princess in Action

Put pictures of your friends on your bathroom mirror.
Whenever you look in the mirror, pray for yourself and
for the people in the pictures.

Growing on the Vine

Royal Words

[Jesus said,] "I am the vine. You are the branches. If anyone remains joined to me, and I to him, he will bear a lot of fruit. You can't do anything without me."

JOHN 15:5

Princess Thoughts

A vine is like a tree trunk. It's long and twisty, and it can have many branches. Grapes grow on the vine branches. The grapes get water to help them grow from the vine. If a branch is cut off, it will die. A well-watered vine, though, will grow lots of grapes. If we stay connected to Jesus, who is called "the vine" in the Bible, we will be able to do many good things.

A Prayer for the King

Thank you, Jesus, for being the vine and helping me to do good things.

Princess in Action

Pretend a rope is a vine. Make some loops in the rope for branches. Have everyone in your family hold on to a loop. Take a walk around the house while holding the rope.

February 10

Growing Big

Royal Words

When you plant the [mustard] seed, it grows. It
becomes the largest of all garden plants. Its branches
are so big that birds can rest in its shade.

Mark 4:32

Princess Thoughts

A mustard seed is one of the tiniest seeds in the world, but it can grow
into a very big and useful plant. Birds can nest in it. Even though you
are little now, you can still do things for God. Even the tiny mustard seed
can be used to make mustard for hot dogs. When you are grown up,
you can do even greater things for God.

A Prayer for the King

Lord, help me to grow and to know how I can do great things
for you now and when I'm a grown-up.

Princess in Action

Talk about how you have grown since you were a baby
and what you have learned to do for God. Plant some
little seeds. Watch them grow.

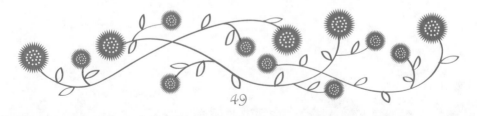

February 11

Growing in Grace

Royal Words

Grow in the grace of our Lord and Savior Jesus Christ. Get
to know him better. Give him glory both now and forever.

2 PETER 3:18

Princess Thoughts

God wants you to know him better. He wants you to grow in
grace and knowledge. That means God wants you to do more
things that make him smile and to learn more about him.
You can do that as you learn the words in the Bible.
Growing this way will make you know and love God more.

A Prayer for the King

Lord, I'm glad you gave me a mind that grows. Help
me to grow closer to you.

Princess in Action

Say some of the Bible verses and stories that you already know.
This shows you are getting to know more about God.

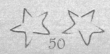

Soft and Hard Hearts

Royal Words

[Pharaoh] would not listen to Moses and Aaron.

EXODUS 9:12, NIV

Princess Thoughts

Pharaoh ruled Egypt when God's people lived there. Pharaoh made the people work for him. He had a hard heart. He was mean to God's people and would not let them leave. Pharaoh wanted the Israelites to keep working for him. God caused lots of problems for Pharaoh until Pharaoh let the people go.

A Prayer for the King

Father, help me to have a soft heart of love for other people. Help me not to be mean and not to have a heart of stone.

Princess in Action

Feel a cold, hard piece of ice. Put it in a bowl and let it melt. Now feel the water. It moves and flows. When you are mean, it's like having a cold, hard heart. When you are nice to others, though, your heart flows with love and you make other people happy.

God Loves and Forgives Me

Royal Words

God is faithful and fair. If we admit that we have sinned, he will forgive us our sins. He will forgive every wrong thing we have done. He will make us pure.

1 JOHN 1:9

Princess Thoughts

God loves you! He knows that sometimes you do things that are wrong. He knows that sometimes you might hurt other people. If you say you're sorry, God will forgive you.

A Prayer for the King

Father God, I'm so happy that you love me and forgive me when I do bad things. Help me to be good.

Princess in Action

With your mom or dad, measure and boil a cup of water. Watch the steam rise and disappear. Measure the water after it cools. The water that turned to steam disappeared! Remember that when God forgives you, your sin disappears.

February 14

Valentine's Day

Royal Words

Jesus said, "Let the little children come to me. Don't keep them away. The kingdom of heaven belongs to people like them."

MATTHEW 19:14

Princess Thoughts

Friends of Jesus tried to stop little children from running up to Jesus. But Jesus told them not to stop the children. Jesus loves all children, including you. You can talk to him anytime.

A Prayer for the King

Jesus, thank you for loving me.

Princess in Action

Make a valentine for Jesus. Color a big paper heart. Have your mom or dad help you write a note on it to Jesus.

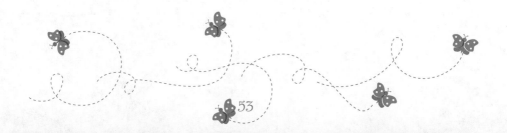

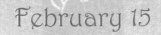

February 15

God's Love Is Deep and Wide

Royal Words

May you have power with all God's people to understand Christ's love. May you know how wide and long and high and deep it is.

EPHESIANS 3:18

Princess Thoughts

Open your hands as wide as you can. God's love is wider! If you stand in your bathtub, you can see how deep the water can get. God's love is deeper. God's love is also higher than the sky and longer than any road. He wants you to know he loves you so much!

A Prayer for the King

Thank you, God, for your love that is deep and wide.

Princess in Action

Use a ruler or tape measure to check out how long, wide, deep, and high things are in your home. Have your mom or dad measure how wide you can stretch your arms. God's love for you is even wider than that!

February 16

Family Love

Royal Words

You will enjoy all of the good things the LORD
your God has given to you and your family.
DEUTERONOMY 26:11

Princess Thoughts

God made families. God wants you to enjoy the people in
your family and all the things you can do together. You can
pray that God will help your family to be happy.

A Prayer for the King

Lord, thank you for making families. Help my family to be happy.

Princess in Action

Look through some of your family's pictures. You could look
at your mom and dad's wedding pictures. Or you could look at
pictures from one of your family vacations. Choose a favorite
picture to keep in your bedroom. Pray for your family every
time you look at the picture.

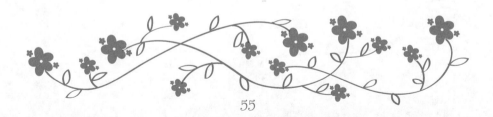

Loving as Jesus Loves

Royal Words

[Jesus said,] "I give you a new command. Love one another. You must love one another, just as I have loved you."

JOHN 13:34

Princess Thoughts

Jesus asks you to love others. He wants you to care about other people and to be kind to them. He wants you to do nice things that show you love people.

A Prayer for the King

Lord, thank you for loving me. Please help me to love all the people you have made.

Princess in Action

Go through your clothes and choose some to give to the poor. Giving to people who have no money for clothes is one way to show that you love them.

February 18

Love That Gives

Royal Words
Some time later God put Abraham to the
test. He said to him, "Abraham!"
"Here I am," Abraham replied.
GENESIS 22:1

Princess Thoughts
God gave Abraham a special kind of test. He asked Abraham
to give up something he treasured, his son. God wants you to
love him more than your toys and more than your best
friends. God should be first in your heart.

A Prayer for the King
Lord, help me to love you more than any of my toys
and friends.

Princess in Action
Is there a toy that you really like to play with? Show
God's love to your brother or sister or friend by sharing
that toy with him or her.

February 19

Hide-and-Seek

Royal Words

[Jochebed] couldn't hide [Moses] any longer. So she got a basket that was made out of the stems of tall grass. She coated it with tar. Then she placed the child in it. She put the basket in the tall grass that grew along the bank of the Nile River.

EXODUS 2:3

Princess Thoughts

Mommy Jochebed worried about her baby because people wanted to hurt him and the other baby boys. First she hid baby Moses in her house. When that didn't work anymore, Mommy Jochebed hid Moses in a little basket that floated in the river. Jochebed hoped that God would protect her son.

A Prayer for the King

Father, thank you for giving me people like my mom, dad, grandparents, and teachers to take care of me.

Princess in Action

Play hide-and-seek with your mom or dad. When you find the person who is hiding, wrap your arms around him or her with a big hug.

February 20

A Watchful Sister

Royal Words

The child's sister [Miriam] wasn't very far away. She
wanted to see what would happen to [Moses].

EXODUS 2:4

Princess Thoughts

While Moses floated in his basket on the river, Miriam, his big sister,
watched what happened to her baby brother. She peeked to see where the
basket would float and who would find it. She wanted Moses to be safe.

A Prayer for the King

Lord, thank you for older brothers, sisters, cousins, and friends who watch
out for me. Help me to take care of children who are younger than me.

Princess in Action

Do you have older brothers or sisters? Thank them for taking
care of you. If you have a younger brother or sister, help your
mom and dad take care of him or her. You can hold his or her
hand on a walk. If you are an only child, write a thank-you
note to an older cousin or friend.

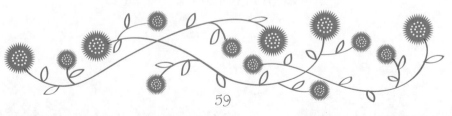

A Princess Finds the Baby

Royal Words

Pharaoh's daughter went down to the Nile River to take a bath. Her attendants were walking along the bank of the river. She saw the basket [with Moses] in the tall grass. So she sent her female slave to get it.

Exodus 2:5

Princess Thoughts

A princess found Moses. She wanted to take him to the palace. Moses' sister, Miriam, asked if the princess needed help with the baby. Miriam said that her mother, Jochebed, could come and help the princess care for Moses. Hooray! God worked things out so Jochebed could be with her baby and he would be safe.

A Prayer for the King

Lord, I trust that you will keep my family and me safe and happy.

Princess in Action

Dress up like a princess and then have a doll hunt. When you find your dolls, hug them.

Praise Parade

Royal Words

Miriam sang to them, "Sing to the LORD. He is greatly honored. He has thrown Pharaoh's horses and their riders into the Red Sea."

EXODUS 15:21

Princess Thoughts

Miriam and Moses grew up. Moses led God's people out of slavery in Egypt. And Miriam felt so happy that she led a parade praising God for freeing his people and answering their prayers.

A Prayer for the King

I thank you, God, for prayers you have answered.

Princess in Action

Have a parade for Jesus. Sing songs about Jesus as you march around the house. Find something you can pretend is a princess's scepter as you march. Shout about a prayer God answered.

February 23

Hiding from God

Royal Words

"Can anyone hide in secret places so that I can't see him?" announces the LORD. "Don't I fill heaven and earth?" announces the LORD.

JEREMIAH 23:24

Princess Thoughts

No matter where you are, God always sees you. You cannot hide from him. Even when you are afraid, God sees you and can take care of you.

A Prayer for the King

Lord, I am happy you always see me and take care of me.

Princess in Action

Play a game of funny places to hide. One person says, "If I could hide in _____" (fill in the blank with crazy places to hide, like in a cloud, inside a straw, or under the sea). Then the other person answers, "God could find you."

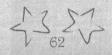

February 24

Kind Words

Royal Words
Sarai treated Hagar badly. So Hagar ran away from her.
GENESIS 16:6

Princess Thoughts
Hagar worked for Sarai. Sarai was mean to Hagar, and finally Hagar ran away. God told Hagar to return to Sarai. He promised that he would bless Hagar's family. No one should be mean to another person. With God's help we can forgive mean people who hurt us. With God's help we can be kind to others.

A Prayer for the King
Lord, help me to forgive people who hurt me. Help me to speak kind words.

Princess in Action
When you are polite, you are being kind to others. Play a please and thank-you game. Think of something to ask for, and remember to say, "Please." Then the other person can do the action and you can say, "Thank you." Try "Please give me a hug" or "Please play a game with me."

February 25

Kindness

Royal Words

Elisha left Jericho and went up to Bethel. He was walking along the road. Some young fellows came out of the town. They made fun of him. "Go on up! You don't even have any hair on your head!" they said.

2 KINGS 2:23

Princess Thoughts

Making fun of someone isn't kind. God wants us to be kind to one another and use words to cheer people up. God does not want us to use words to hurt other people.

A Prayer for the King

Lord, help me to use words to make people feel good.

Princess in Action

When someone teases you, remember that God loves you. You are his princess. Use words to help people feel good. Tell your mom she looks pretty or that she's smart. Tell your dad that he is strong and that he is kind.

Greetings

Royal Words

When all the people saw Jesus, they were filled
with wonder. And they ran to greet him.

MARK 9:15

Princess Thoughts

A crowd of people saw Jesus and ran to greet him. A greeting
is how we say hello and welcome someone. When you are
excited to see someone, you probably run to meet him or her,
or maybe you jump up and down with joy. The people in the
Bible story were excited to see Jesus.

A Prayer for the King

Hi, Jesus. I'm happy you are here with me and listening to me.

Princess in Action

Practice opening the door and greeting people when they
come to your house. Greet Jesus in the morning by saying,
"Good morning, Jesus. I am glad you are here with me."

Powerful Prayer

Royal Words

The prayer of a godly person is powerful.
It makes things happen.

JAMES 5:16

Princess Thoughts

When we pray to God, the King, he listens to us. We can ask him to heal us when we're sick. Or we can ask him to help us feel happy when we're sad. When we pray, God uses his power to answer.

A Prayer for the King

Lord, help me to practice my praying.

Princess in Action

Is there something you want to pray to God about today? Practice praying to him. If you pray every day, you will become a great pray-er.

February 28

Prayer Walk

Royal Words

Enoch walked with God 300 years after Methuselah [his
son] was born. He also had other sons and daughters.

GENESIS 5:22

Princess Thoughts

Adam and Eve had a great-great-great-great-grandson
named Enoch. The Bible tells us that Enoch walked
with God. This means that Enoch obeyed God and
talked with God every day. God walks with you. He
is always with you and goes where you go.

A Prayer for the King

Father, I am thankful you walk with me. Help me to follow you.

Princess in Action

Bundle up and take a walk outside with an adult. Talk to
God as you go. Use your arms and hands to point at all
the things God has made. Talk to God about the colors,
plants, and animals you see.

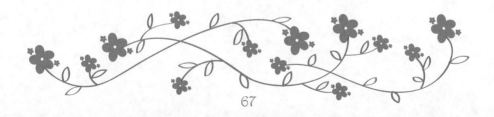

March

Beautiful Hands

Royal Words

May the favor of the Lord our God rest on us; establish the work of our hands for us—yes, establish the work of our hands.
Psalm 90:17, niv

Princess Thoughts

Look at the hands God gave you. They have fingers that wiggle and thumbs that make it easy for you to pick up objects and make things. We choose how we use our hands. We can use them to hurt someone else (that's a bad choice) or to help someone (that's a good choice).

A Prayer for the King

Father King, thank you for my hands. Help me use them to help others.

Princess in Action

Choose ways to use your hands to help someone. Make a list of ways to help others with your hands. See how many of them you can do today. You could help your mom or dad set the table for a meal. You could wave hello to your neighbor.

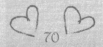

Too Much Stuff

Royal Words

The land didn't have enough food for both of them.
They had large herds and many servants. So they weren't
able to stay together.

Genesis 13:6

Princess Thoughts

Long ago Abram and his nephew, Lot, noticed a problem.
They had so much stuff that it caused them to fight over
where to keep everything. So the men moved away from each
other. Do you have too many toys and clothes and not
enough room for all of it? Your parents may always have
to tell you to clean your toys up. You don't have to move.
Give some of your things away to make more room.

A Prayer for the King

Lord, thank you for my toys and clothes. Help me to give
away what I no longer need.

Princess in Action

Sort out your clothes and toys. Give away what you don't use
or clothes that don't fit anymore. Make room before asking
for more toys or clothes.

Princess Prayers

Royal Words

I will praise you [God] as long as I live. I will
lift up my hands when I pray to you.

PSALM 63:4

Princess Thoughts

Before David became king of Israel, he was a shepherd
caring for sheep. For a time, he also lived in a desert. He
was running away from a king who wanted to hurt him.
At last David moved to a palace. David prayed
everywhere he lived. He lifted his hands to the sky
toward heaven and prayed. David knew that every day
is a great day to talk to God.

A Prayer for the King

Dear God, I'm happy you like to listen to me every day.

Princess in Action

Hold your hands up high, and spread your arms wide. Look
up. Tell God about your day. Let him know that you are
happy you are his princess. He will listen.

Faith Walk, Hand in Hand

Royal Words

The commandments I give you today must be in your hearts. Make sure your children learn them. Talk about them when you are at home. Talk about them when you walk along the road. Speak about them when you go to bed. And speak about them when you get up.

DEUTERONOMY 6:6-7

Princess Thoughts

God wants moms and dads to talk to their children about obeying God. He likes us to talk to our parents when we walk, sit, travel, or stay home. God wants to be part of our whole lives.

A Prayer for the King

Father King, I like hearing about you. Help me to remember you every day.

Princess in Action

Take a faith walk with your mom or dad. Hold hands and talk about God as you walk. Share your favorite Bible stories or answers to prayer as you walk.

Helping the Sick

Royal Words

After the crowd had been sent outside, Jesus went in.
He took the girl by the hand, and she got up.

MATTHEW 9:25

Princess Thoughts

Jesus visited a girl who was very sick. Jesus said, "She is
asleep." He touched her hand, and she sat up. Then she
stood. Hooray! Jesus had healed the girl and made her
healthy again.

A Prayer for the King

Dear Lord Jesus, I am happy you care about girls
and want us to be healthy.

Princess in Action

Send a card to a sick friend. Say a prayer for Jesus
to make the person well.

March 6

Sharing with Jesus

Royal Words
[A disciple of Jesus] said, "Here is a boy with five small
loaves of barley bread. He also has two small fish.
But how far will that go in such a large crowd?"
JOHN 6:9

Princess Thoughts
A little boy shared his lunch with Jesus, and a wonderful
miracle happened. Jesus blessed the food, and the fish
and bread the boy had brought became enough to feed a
huge crowd of people. Jesus fed many hungry people and
stopped the growling in their tummies.

A Prayer for the King
Dear Father, thank you for taking care of people who are hungry.

Princess in Action
Ask your mom or dad for cans of food you could give to
a food pantry. A food pantry passes the food out to poor
people who need it. When you feed the hungry, you are
helping Jesus feed people.

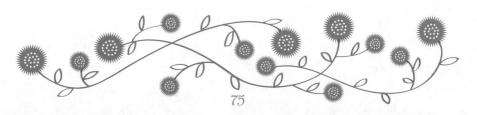

Healthy Foods

Royal Words
After the ten days they looked healthy and well fed. In fact, they looked better than any of the young men who ate the king's food.
DANIEL 1:15

Princess Thoughts
Daniel worked in the king's palace but didn't want to eat the king's food. He didn't want to drink what the king drank, either. Instead, Daniel wanted to eat lots of vegetables and drink water. After eating the vegetables for over a week, Daniel and his friends looked healthier than the people who ate the king's food.

A Prayer for the King
Father King, thanks for the vegetables you created. Help me to eat food that is good for me.

Princess in Action
Make your table pretty, fit for a princess, by helping to set it. Fold the napkins. Put forks and spoons at each place. Wear clean clothes when you sit to eat. Make sure to eat all the vegetables on your plate!

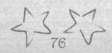

March 8

A Beautiful Robe

Royal Words

Israel loved Joseph more than any of his other
sons. Joseph had been born to him when he was
old. Israel made him a beautiful robe.

GENESIS 37:3

Princess Thoughts

Joseph's daddy loved him very much. So Joseph's daddy
gave him a beautiful robe. A robe is a type of coat. This
one had many colors on it. It sounds like a wonderful
present. God loves all of his children very much.

A Prayer for the King

God, thank you for loving me and giving me beautiful clothes.

Princess in Action

Put on your coat, and thank your mom and dad for your
beautiful robe.

Baby Clothes

Royal Words

[The angel said,] "Here is how you will know I am telling you the truth. You will find a baby wrapped in strips of cloth and lying in a manger."

LUKE 2:12

Princess Thoughts

Jesus wasn't born in a hospital. He was born in a barn. Mary, his mom, didn't have a fancy blanket, so she wrapped baby Jesus in scraps of cloth. Jesus slept in a manger, not a crib. A manger held food for animals. When the angel told the shepherds about Jesus, the angel said the shepherds would find him wrapped in strips of cloth, lying in a manger.

A Prayer for the King

Thank you, Father, that I have a home and a bed where I can sleep.

Princess in Action

Wrap your doll in a towel or blanket like the cloths Mary wrapped around Jesus. That was the first robe King Jesus wore.

March 10

New Clothes

Royal Words

Each year [Samuel's] mother made him a little robe. She took
it to him when she went up to Shiloh with her husband.

1 SAMUEL 2:19

Princess Thoughts

As a little boy, Samuel helped in the Tabernacle, which was
like a church in Bible times. He lived in the temple, so his
mother did not see him often. She loved him and wove a new
robe for him every year. Moms are special and take care of
making or buying clothes for their children.

A Prayer for the King

Thank you, God, for giving me a mommy who takes
care of my clothes.

Princess in Action

Show you are thankful to have clothes by taking care of them.
Hang your clothes up, or put your clothes in drawers. Don't drop
them on the floor and step on them. Put dirty clothes in a basket
or in the place your mom wants them to go.

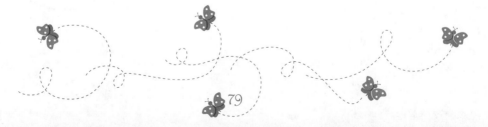

Fairness

Royal Words
I put on a godly life as if it were my clothes.
Fairness was my robe and my turban.
JOB 29:14

Princess Thoughts
People who are fair treat everyone honestly and with respect. Job said being fair was like putting on clothes. He tried to put on fairness every day. His actions were better than a beautiful robe.

A Prayer for the King
Dear Father King, you are always fair and loving.
Help me to be fair too.

Princess in Action
Play dress up. Put on clothes that a mommy wears. Put on fairness, too, by sharing your dress-up clothes with a friend.

March 12

Honoring Someone

Royal Words

Give the robe and horse to one of your most noble princes. Let the
robe be put on the man you want to honor. Let him be led on the
horse through the city streets. Let people announce in front of him,
"This is what is done for the man the king wants to honor!"

ESTHER 6:9

Princess Thoughts

To honor someone is to do something to show that the person
is special. Mordecai saved the king's life, so the king wanted
to honor him. The king let Mordecai wear his robe. He told
Haman to parade Mordecai through the streets, telling the
people how Mordecai saved the king's life.

A Prayer for the King

Dear Father King, help me to honor people who love you.
They are special.

Princess in Action

Think of someone who did something special for Jesus or for
you, a princess. Maybe your dad drove you to church or a
friend shared her toys. Think of a special way to thank that
person. Your action will show honor.

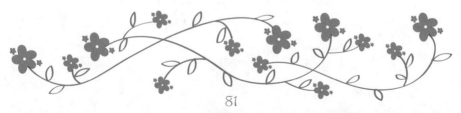

Clothes That Smell Good

Royal Words

Myrrh and aloes and cassia make all of your robes smell good.
Psalm 45:8

Princess Thoughts

These words talk about Jesus. He wears a sweet-smelling robe.
Myrrh is a plant with a sweet smell, like a perfume. Aloes are
a family of plants that can be made into soap. Cassia is
another name for a cinnamon plant. Smell cinnamon, soap,
and perfumes. Smell your clothes. Do they smell good?
Clean clothes smell good.

A Prayer for the King

Dear Lord God, thanks for making plants that smell good.
Thank you for soap that cleans our clothes.

Princess in Action

Help your mom or dad wash clothes. Put clothes in the washer
and help add the soap. Smell the laundry detergent.
Check how clothes smell before
and after being washed.

March 14

A Robe for God

Royal Words

You [God] wrap yourself in light as if it were a robe.
You spread the heavens out like a tent.

PSALM 104:2

Princess Thoughts

The Bible tells us that God wears a robe. His robe is a little
different from our clothes, though. God sparkles like sunshine.
He made light and hung the sun and stars in the sky.

A Prayer for the King

Dear Father, I like the sunshine you made. When I play
on a sunny day, I can think of you.

Princess in Action

Play outside, and look up to the sky. Think about the light
surrounding God. At night, go outside with your mom or dad
and look at the stars. Try to find the Little Dipper.

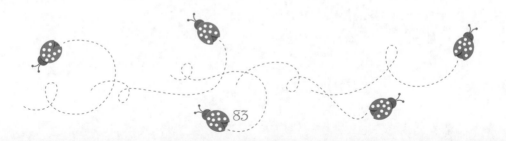

A Woman Who Sewed

Royal Words

When [Peter] arrived, he was taken upstairs to the room. All the widows stood around him crying. They showed him the robes and other clothes Dorcas had made while she was still alive.

ACTS 9:39

Princess Thoughts

When Dorcas died, many of her friends cried. They loved her and remembered how she sewed clothes for them, including robes. Peter prayed, and God brought Dorcas back to life. God answered the prayers with a miracle. Hooray! Dorcas could sew for her friends and people in need again.

A Prayer for the King

Dear Father, thank you for the people who give me clothes. Please keep them healthy and safe.

Princess in Action

Remember the people who give you beautiful clothes. Have someone take a picture of you wearing pretty clothes. Thank the people who gave you those clothes, and give them a picture of you wearing the clothes. Pray for the people who give you dresses, tops, and even socks.

March 16

Generous Jonathan

Royal Words

Jonathan took off the robe he was wearing and gave it to David. He also gave him his military clothes. He even gave him his sword, his bow and his belt.

1 Samuel 18:4

Princess Thoughts

A weapon is among the most important objects a soldier owns. Jonathan gave his sword away to his friend David because David needed one. Jonathan also gave David the coat he wore. He loved his friend so much that he helped when he saw what his friend needed.

A Prayer for the King

Lord, help me to love my friends. Show me how I can help them when they need help.

Princess in Action

When someone visits, share what you have. Offer your friend a snack or a drink. See if you can tell if your friend needs anything. Talk to your mom or dad about giving the person a special toy or book that you like.

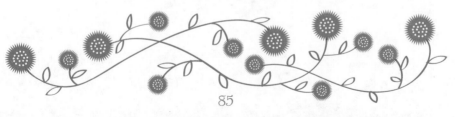

Cheerful Givers

Royal Words
You should each give what you have decided in your heart to give. You shouldn't give if you don't want to. You shouldn't give because you are forced to. God loves a cheerful giver.
2 CORINTHIANS 9:7

Princess Thoughts
A princess has a heart that is generous and cheerful. To be generous means to be happy to share and give gifts to other people. God will not force you to give or share toys, food, or anything else. He is happy when you choose to be generous.

A Prayer for the King
Dear Father, I want a heart that is happy to share.

Princess in Action
Think of what you can share today. If you have saved some money, you could choose to give some of it to Jesus in the church offering.

Generous People

Royal Words

She opens her arms to those who are poor. She reaches out her hands to those who are needy.

PROVERBS 31:20

Princess Thoughts

Today's Bible verse describes an important woman who does many good deeds. She is a mother and a wife. She is also a princess, just like you are a princess. As a princess she cares for people in need. She is generous, and that means she is happy to share what she has with other people, especially the poor.

A Prayer for the King

Dear Father King, thank you for my mom, who is a princess and a special lady because she takes care of me and my family. Help me to be generous, just like my mom is generous.

Princess in Action

You can be generous at home. Ask your mom if there is a chore you can help her with. When playing a game, let your brother or sister or friend take a turn first.

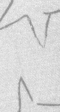

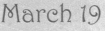

God's Special Children

Royal Words

[Jesus said,] "Anyone who welcomes a little child
like this in my name welcomes me."
MATTHEW 18:5

Princess Thoughts

Friends of Jesus asked, "Who will be the greatest in
heaven?" But instead of answering the question right
away, Jesus asked a child to stand next to him and talked
about welcoming children. He reminded his friends to
care about children. Jesus loves children. Welcome your
friends and other children you meet.

A Prayer for the King

Father King, thank you for loving me. I am special to you.
Help me to love other people.

Princess in Action

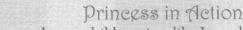

You can welcome children, just like Jesus did. Be nice to new
children in your Sunday school class at church. Ask them
to play with you. Sit next to them during the lesson.
Smile whenever you see another child
because each person is special to God.

Touch

Royal Words

People were bringing little children to Jesus.
They wanted him to touch them.

MARK 10:13

Princess Thoughts

The people knew Jesus loved children. They wanted the children
to meet Jesus. Jesus gave them a gentle touch, like a little pat or a
hug. A good touch is like petting a kitten or giving a friend a high
five. Hitting or pushing someone is a bad touch.

A Prayer for the King

Father, help me to be gentle and show people kindness
with a good touch.

Princess in Action

Use your hands to give a good touch to people and
animals. Give high fives to your mommy or daddy.
Pat your pets or stuffed animals.

Saved by a Queen

Royal Words

Queen Esther answered, "King Xerxes, I hope you will show me your favor. I hope you will be pleased to let me live. That's what I want. Please spare my people. That's my appeal to you."

ESTHER 7:3

Princess Thoughts

Queen Esther could only speak to the king if he asked her to. If he didn't ask her to speak, and she tried to talk to him, she could get into big trouble. Enemies planned to hurt Esther's people. So she bravely asked the king to save the people she loved. The king stopped the plan to hurt the people. The people were safe. Hooray!

A Prayer for the King

Dear Father King, keep my family safe.
Protect the people I love.

Princess in Action

Soldiers fight to keep us safe. If you know a soldier, draw a picture and send it to him or her.

March 22

The King's Touch

Royal Words
Jesus came and touched [the disciples].
"Get up," he said. "Don't be afraid."
MATTHEW 17:7

Princess Thoughts
When the disciples heard God speak from heaven, they were
scared. But Jesus touched his friends and calmed them down.
He wanted them to remember that he was with them and
cared for them. Jesus is with you, too.

A Prayer for the King
Lord Jesus, thank you for being with me. Help me to
trust you and not be afraid.

Princess in Action
When you are afraid, touch your Bible to remember that Jesus is
with you. If your friend is scared, give him or her a hug.

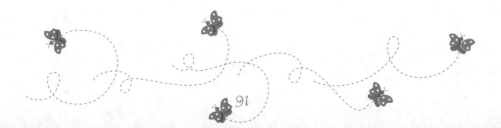

Doing Nothing

Royal Words

God loved the world so much that he gave his one
and only Son. Anyone who believes in him
will not die but will have eternal life.

JOHN 3:16

Princess Thoughts

Some people think they have to do a lot of good things in
order to go to heaven. But we don't have to work our way to
heaven. All we need to do is believe that Jesus died for us and
ask him to forgive us for the bad things we've done. He died
on the cross so we could go to heaven.

A Prayer for the King

Lord Jesus, thank you for dying for me so that I can
be with you in heaven someday.

Princess in Action

Have you thanked Jesus for dying on the cross for your sins?
Have you asked him to forgive you for the bad things you
have done? If you have, hooray! You will
go to heaven and be a princess forever.

Watch Your Heart

Royal Words

Above everything else, guard your heart.
It is where your life comes from.

PROVERBS 4:23

Princess Thoughts

Blood flows through your heart to keep you alive. Your heart is
also the center for your feelings, like happiness and sadness. God
warns us to watch our hearts. That means to keep out anger,
selfishness, and other bad feelings. It also means to let in love,
forgiveness, and other good feelings.

A Prayer for the King

Father King, thank you for my heart. Please help me to let
good feelings stay in my heart.

Princess in Action

Learn to put your fingers on your throat or wrist to feel your heart
beating. Each beat happens because blood is flowing from your
heart through your body.

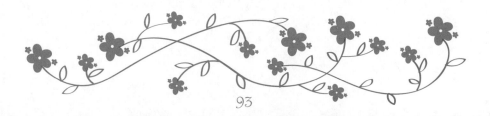

Clean Feet

Royal Words
"Lord," Simon Peter replied, "not just my feet!
Wash my hands and my head too!"
JOHN 13:9

Princess Thoughts
The disciples walked on dirt roads, so their feet got really
dirty. One special night, Jesus washed the disciples' feet.
Peter tried to stop Jesus. But Jesus said that if Peter wanted to
be with him, he had to let Jesus wash his feet. Peter really
wanted to be with Jesus, so he asked Jesus to wash his hands
and his head, too. But Jesus said Peter had already had a bath
and he only needed to wash his feet.

A Prayer for the King
Lord Jesus, I want to be with you too. I am happy
to let you help me.

Princess in Action
Look at your hands and feet. Are they dirty?
If so, wash them or let your mommy or daddy wash them.
Use soap that helps get rid of germs.

Thirty Coins

Royal Words

[Judas] asked, "What will you give me if I hand Jesus over to you?" So they counted out 30 silver coins for him.

MATTHEW 26:15

Princess Thoughts

The high priests wanted to know where Jesus was. They wanted to arrest Jesus. Judas, one of the disciples, told the high priests where they could find Jesus. As a reward, the high priests gave Judas only a little money. It was the same price they paid for a slave. Oh no! Judas sold Jesus like a slave. Judas hurt his friend.

A Prayer for the King

Father King, I do not want to hurt Jesus. Help me believe in Jesus and tell others about him.

Princess in Action

Ask your mommy or daddy to help you count thirty coins. Some may be silver, like a dime or quarter. Talk about what you could buy at a store with the money. How long would that item last? Would it be worth hurting a friend over?

March 27

A Robe for Jesus

Royal Words
They took off his clothes and put a purple robe on him.
MATTHEW 27:28

Princess Thoughts
It sounds nice that people put a purple robe on Jesus, but
these people didn't want to be nice. They teased Jesus
and laughed at him. They didn't believe God the Father
sent Jesus to save us or that Jesus really is a king. Jesus
understood and asked God the Father to forgive the
people who hurt him. A real king forgives people.

A Prayer for the King
Lord Jesus, thank you for forgiving the people who hurt you.
Help me to forgive people who are mean to me.

Princess in Action
Wear purple today to remember that Jesus is the
King. If people tease you or are mean, remember
that you are a princess and forgive them.

A Sad Day

Royal Words

With the help of evil people, you put Jesus to
death. You nailed him to the cross.

ACTS 2:23

Princess Thoughts

People nailed Jesus to a cross. Jesus died. Jesus chose to
die so that people who ask him for forgiveness for their
sins can go to heaven.

A Prayer for the King

Dear Jesus, thank you for dying on the cross so I can
go to heaven.

Princess in Action

Jesus was strong and brave to die on the cross for us.
Let your mommy or daddy help you use a hammer to hit
a nail into a piece of wood. You could hammer two
pieces of wood together to make a cross. *Bang, bang!*
It takes a hard whack to hit the nail into the wood.
Thank Jesus for dying for you.

Alive!

Royal Words

[Jesus said,] "It is really I! . . ." After he said that,
he showed them his hands and feet.

LUKE 24:39-40

Princess Thoughts

Jesus came back to life. He didn't stay dead. Hooray! His
friends thought they saw a ghost until Jesus showed them the
scars on his hands and feet and let them watch him eat fish.
He could move, eat, and talk with his friends again.

A Prayer for the King

Lord Jesus, it's wonderful news that you came back to life!

Princess in Action

You are alive! Look at your hands and feet. Wiggle your
toes and fingers. Lift your pretty hands high up and
shout, "Jesus is risen!"

A Royal Robe

Royal Words

[Jesus] will be dressed in majesty as if it were his
royal robe. He will sit as king on his throne.

ZECHARIAH 6:13

Princess Thoughts

Once upon a time, long before Jesus came as a baby, God the
Father told people about Jesus. God the Father called Jesus the
Messiah. God the Father said that Jesus would sit on a throne like
a king. If you are a Christian, you will see that in heaven one day.

A Prayer for the King

Dear Lord Jesus, you are a king in heaven.
Thank you for asking me to be your princess.

Princess in Action

Use a twist tie to put together two sticks, or cinnamon sticks,
to form a cross. If you use plain sticks, spray them with perfume.
Decorate it with a purple ribbon. Smell the cross.
It's sweet. Jesus is our sweet King.

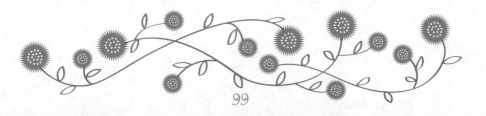

White Robes

Royal Words

I looked, and there in front of me was a huge crowd
of people. They stood in front of the throne and in
front of the Lamb. There were so many that no one
could count them. They came from every nation, tribe,
people and language. They were wearing white robes.
In their hands they were holding palm branches.

REVELATION 7:9

Princess Thoughts

Wow! Lots of people will be in heaven all dressed in white
robes. They will be from every country in the world. All these
people will worship Jesus, also called the Lamb, who will sit
on his throne in heaven.

A Prayer for the King

Father God, I am so happy that heaven is big
enough for everyone who believes in you.

Princess in Action

Wear white today to remind you of all the people who
will be in heaven. Tell people there's lots of room in
heaven for everyone.

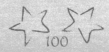

April

Springtime Flowers

Royal Words

Flowers are appearing on the earth. The season for singing has come. The cooing of doves is heard in our land.

SONG OF SONGS 2:12

Princess Thoughts

God made the sweet-smelling flowers. In the spring, flowers start to bloom. Birds that flew south for the winter return and tweet little songs.

A Prayer for the King

Father King, you made beautiful flowers and birds that sing. Thank you.

Princess in Action

Take a flower walk. Look for signs of springtime and flowers that are budding or blooming. Listen for birds. Thank God for each flower you find and the birds you hear.

Party for Jesus

Royal Words

The Wise Men went to the house. There they saw
the child with his mother Mary. They bowed down
and worshiped him. Then they opened their treasures.
They gave him gold, incense and myrrh.

MATTHEW 2:11

Princess Thoughts

After the birth of Jesus, wise men came and gave him gifts. Incense
and myrrh are like sweet-smelling perfumes. Gold costs a lot of
money. The wise men bowed and worshiped Jesus, the new King.

A Prayer for the King

Lord Jesus, you are special. You are a King and deserve
the gift of my love.

Princess in Action

Have a spring party for Jesus. If you can, pick or buy sweet-
smelling flowers for Jesus. Or draw a picture of flowers. Make
cupcakes, and put a candle in one. Let an adult light the candle.
Sing a praise song. Dance for Jesus.

Sweet Scents

Royal Words

Mary took about a pint of pure nard. It was an expensive perfume. She poured it on Jesus' feet and wiped them with her hair. The house was filled with the sweet smell of the perfume.

JOHN 12:3

Princess Thoughts

This Mary is not the mother of Jesus. This Mary made bad choices until she met Jesus. He forgave her for the bad things she did. Then she followed Jesus and made better choices. She poured nard, a very expensive perfume, on the feet of Jesus so that he would smell pretty. She used her hair as a towel. *Sniff. Sniff.* The whole house smelled sweet.

A Prayer for the King

Lord Jesus, thanks for saving women like Mary. Thank you for forgiving us. That's better than perfume.

Princess in Action

Make your feet smell better by rubbing body lotion on them. Here's an idea for you to do with your mommy or daddy to make shoes smell better. Put loose tea leaves and a pinch of cinnamon into an old sock. Close the opening of the sock with a rubber band. Slip the sock into a shoe when it is off your foot.

Sweet Friends

Royal Words

Perfume and incense bring joy to your heart. And a
friend is sweeter when he gives you honest advice.
PROVERBS 27:9

Princess Thoughts

Sweet smells are pleasant. A good friend is even better
than sweet perfumes. A good friend tells the truth
and wants the best for her friend.

A Prayer for the King

Father King, thanks for making sweet-smelling flowers and fruits
that we use to make perfume. Thanks for giving me good friends.
Help me to be a good friend.

Princess in Action

Ask your mommy if you can smell some of her perfumes.
Talk about sweet words to say to a friend. Invite a friend to play,
and say sweet words to your friend.

Sweet Life That Lasts

Royal Words

God considers us to be the sweet smell that Christ is spreading among people who are being saved and people who are dying.

2 CORINTHIANS 2:15

Princess Thoughts

We can add bubble bath to water in a tub and use sweet-smelling shampoo on our hair to smell good. But God is talking about a different scent. It's a sweet smell of life. When you walk outside in the spring, the air smells fresh because there's new life growing. People who believe in Christ bring the hope of a spring that lasts forever. The sweet smell is a reminder of the new life of believers who will live in heaven forever.

A Prayer for the King

Lord Jesus, thanks for saving me and helping me bring a sweet smell of life to people.

Princess in Action

Take a bubble bath. You'll be clean and smell sweet. When you go out, smile and tell people about Jesus so they can have a new life in heaven one day.

Sweet Water

Royal Words

When [a tree] smells water, it will begin to grow.
It will send out new growth like a plant.

Job 14:9

Princess Thoughts

Seeds and plants need water to grow. The plant's roots actually
smell the water and grow toward it to drink it up. The plant sucks
in the water, and the water helps the plant to grow.

A Prayer for the King

Father King, thanks for making beautiful plants and trees.

Princess in Action

Water some plants and trees around your home. Hunt for buds
that show the plant will blossom soon.

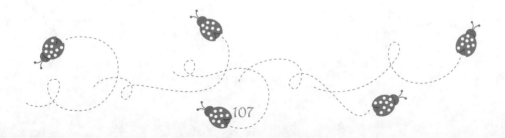

Sweet-Smelling Bread

Royal Words

Mix [flour] with olive oil. Grill it on a metal plate.
Break it in pieces. Bring it as a grain offering. It
gives a smell that is pleasant to [the Lord].

LEVITICUS 6:21

Princess Thoughts

Today's Bible verse is about making bread and offering it to
God. Warm bread in the oven is a good smell. God likes
people to work and give him part of what they make.

A Prayer for the King

Lord God, thanks for giving me energy to work. Help me
to do what makes you happy.

Princess in Action

Help your mom or dad make bread for the homeless or a
family in need as a way to give to God. Smell the bread,
and think of how God will smile
when you give the bread to someone.

April 8

Talking Stick

Royal Words

We hear that some people among you don't want to work.
They aren't really busy. Instead, they are bothering others.

2 Thessalonians 3:11

Princess Thoughts

Sometimes a person who isn't working and feels bored
bothers people who are working. Sometimes the person wants
to get attention. Sometimes the person is nosy and wants to
see what everyone else is doing. The Bible says these people
are busybodies (NIV).

A Prayer for the King

Father King, help me to not be a busybody.

Princess in Action

Decorate a stick to be a talking stick. Use it as a silent signal.
If your dad and mom look busy, place the talking stick near
them. The stick can be a reminder to come and talk with
you after their work is finished.

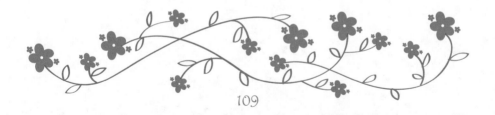

A Holy Throne

Royal Words

God rules over the nations. He is seated on his holy throne.
PSALM 47:8

Princess Thoughts

God is our King. He sits on a throne. It's not just any throne.
It's a holy throne in heaven. God is holy. That means he
is perfect and never does anything wrong.

A Prayer for the King

Father God, I am happy to know you are perfect and holy.
Thank you for being a good king who loves me.

Princess in Action

Keep the chairs in your home looking good for God the King.
Any chair can become a throne. Dust chairs to make them
clean for sitting. Sit and talk to God.

April 10

Always Seen

Royal Words

The Lord is in his holy temple. The Lord is on his throne in heaven. He watches all people. His eyes study them.

PSALM 11:4

Princess Thoughts

God sits on a throne in heaven and watches you. He even studies you. That means he pays attention and notices all the things you do. He looks at your smiles and your frowns. He knows when you are happy or sad.

A Prayer for the King

Father King, thank you for watching over me, understanding my feelings, and always loving me.

Princess in Action

Look at a doll or stuffed animal you like through a magnifying glass. You can see tiny details. God sees every detail about you.

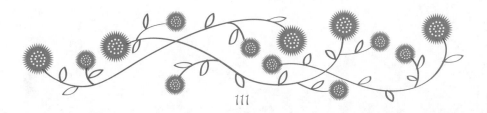

April 11

Wiggles for Joy

Royal Words
May these thoughts of mine please [my God].
I find my joy in the LORD.
PSALM 104:34

Princess Thoughts
God knows what you are thinking. You can sit or stand.
You can run or jump. God still knows your thoughts.
Always think good thoughts.

A Prayer for the King
Father God, I'm happy you know what I think no matter
what I'm doing. That means I can always talk to you.

Princess in Action
Think a nice thought about God. He knows what you
just thought! Run around, jump up and down, and
wiggle while you think about God. He knows those
thoughts too.

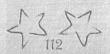

A Royal Family

Royal Words

You are all children of God by believing in Christ Jesus.
GALATIANS 3:26

Princess Thoughts

God is the King. Anyone who believes in Jesus is God's child. That means that people who believe in Jesus are princesses and princes. Believers are part of one big family.

A Prayer for the King

Father King, thanks for being my heavenly daddy.

Princess in Action

Dress up, and sit on a special chair. You can even wear a crown. Let someone take your picture. When you look at the picture, you can remember that you are God's princess.

Beloved Princess

Royal Words

You are the children that God dearly
loves. So be just like him.

EPHESIANS 5:1

Princess Thoughts

God loves you very much and wants you to be like him. He loves
everyone. He is kind. He cares about each person.

A Prayer for the King

Father King, thank you for loving me so much. Help me to share
your love and to be like you.

Princess in Action

Cut out a paper heart. Tape it to the chair you sit in at meals.
The paper heart can be a reminder that God loves you.
Be polite and kind as you eat. At the end of the meal, hug
each person sitting at the table.

A Wise Leader

Royal Words

[King Solomon] made a large throne. It was decorated with ivory. It was covered with fine gold.

1 Kings 10:18

Princess Thoughts

Solomon was one of God's special people. He ruled Israel as a king. He sat on a beautiful throne. God gave Solomon great wisdom to lead Israel. That means God helped Solomon make good choices.

A Prayer for the King

Dear Father, thank you for our leaders. Give them wisdom to lead this country well.

Princess in Action

Draw a big crown on paper. Tape the crown on a chair, and pretend you're sitting on a throne. Sit there as a princess and pray. Ask Jesus to help you make good choices like Solomon did.

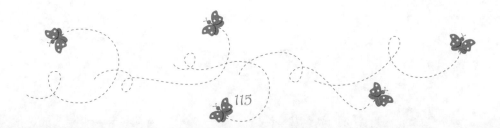

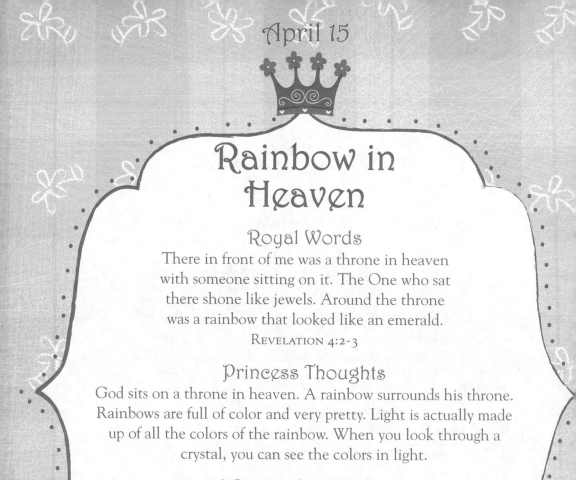

Rainbow in Heaven

Royal Words

There in front of me was a throne in heaven
with someone sitting on it. The One who sat
there shone like jewels. Around the throne
was a rainbow that looked like an emerald.

REVELATION 4:2-3

Princess Thoughts

God sits on a throne in heaven. A rainbow surrounds his throne.
Rainbows are full of color and very pretty. Light is actually made
up of all the colors of the rainbow. When you look through a
crystal, you can see the colors in light.

A Prayer for the King

Father King, thanks for making pretty rainbows.

Princess in Action

Make a paper rainbow to hang up as a reminder that
there's a rainbow in heaven.

Hugs for Jesus

Royal Words

Jesus took a little child and had the child stand among them. Then he took the child in his arms.

MARK 9:36

Princess Thoughts

Jesus loves children. In the Bible, he prayed for children. He hugged them too. Jesus is a king who really cares about his people.

A Prayer for the King

Lord Jesus, thank you for loving everyone, including children like me.

Princess in Action

Send hugs to Jesus. Wrap your arms across your chest, and squeeze your arms to make a hug. Look up and open your arms high and wide to send the hug to Jesus.

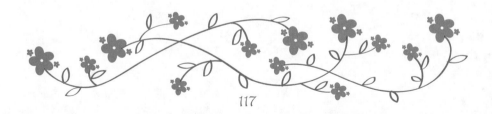

Sitting with the King

Royal Words

[Jesus said,] "I'll give those who overcome the right to sit with me on my throne. In the same way, I overcame. Then I sat down with my Father on his throne."

REVELATION 3:21

Princess Thoughts

Jesus is God's Son, and he has a throne next to God's throne. Jesus sits with God the Father in heaven. Although you can't see him, Jesus sits with you, too. He will always be with you.

A Prayer for the King

Lord Jesus, thanks for loving me and sitting with me. I will never be alone.

Princess in Action

Hooray! Jesus sits on the throne, and he sits with you. Sit down and tell Jesus about your day. He can hear everything you say, even the tiniest whisper.

God Hears Our Prayers

Royal Words
God sits on his throne forever. He hears my prayers.
PSALM 55:19

Princess Thoughts
Good listeners stop what they are doing, look at you,
and pay attention to what you are saying. God does that.
He listens to your prayers.

A Prayer for the King
Father King, thanks for always listening to my prayers.

Princess in Action
Sit and talk to God. Tell him what makes you happy. Tell him
what makes you sad. Thank him for your favorite toy.
Your words to him are prayers. He hears you.

April 19

Sweet Prayers

Royal Words

May my prayer come to you like the sweet smell
of incense. When I lift up my hands in prayer,
may it be like the evening sacrifice.

PSALM 141:2

Princess Thoughts

Prayers are sweet to God. Praying to God is like sending
sweet perfume to him. God loves it when we pray to him.

A Prayer for the King

Dear Father God, may my prayers sound sweet to you
and be like a sweet perfume.

Princess in Action

Smell cinnamon and other spices. To God, your prayers
smell as good as the spices. Take some time to pray.
Begin with saying good things about God. Thank him
for loving you. Then tell him about things that you
need. Ask him for help.

Mercy

Royal Words

Let us boldly approach the throne of grace. Then we will receive mercy. We will find grace to help us when we need it.

HEBREWS 4:16

Princess Thoughts

God is very powerful, but he loves us. He wants us to come to him and talk to him. Mercy means to treat someone with kindness even if he or she has done something bad. Because of mercy, God forgives us.

A Prayer for the King

Father King, thank you for loving me even when I do something bad. Thank you for your mercy.

Princess in Action

Sit and talk to God. Tell him you are sorry if you disobeyed a rule or hurt someone. Ask him to forgive you. Then thank him for forgiving you.

Special Words

Royal Words

You [Timothy] have known the Holy Scriptures ever
since you were a little child. They are able to teach
you how to be saved by believing in Christ Jesus.

2 TIMOTHY 3:15

Princess Thoughts

Timothy believed in Jesus since he was a child. He learned
the Scriptures as a little boy and still remembered them
when he grew up. That's marvelous.

A Prayer for the King

Father God, your words in the Bible teach me about following you
and about your love. Thanks for giving us the Bible.

Princess in Action

The words in the Bible are special. Repeat today's verse to
remember it. You can choose other verses to memorize too.
Ask your mommy or daddy when they
first learned about Jesus.

April 22

Sharing and Understanding

Royal Words

"How can I [understand]?" he said. "I need someone to explain it to me." So he invited Philip to come up and sit with him.

ACTS 8:31

Princess Thoughts

A man who didn't know Jesus read the Bible. He didn't understand what he had read. The man met Philip and asked him to sit down and explain the verses. Philip did that, and the man soon became a Christian.

A Prayer for the King

Father King, help me to share what I know about you so that other people will love you too.

Princess in Action

It's good to share about Jesus. Tell your friend a Bible verse. Or sing a song about Jesus. Tell your friend that Jesus loves both of you.

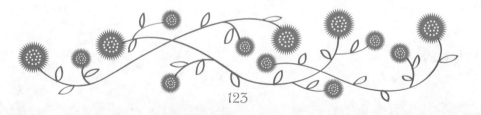

Decisions

Royal Words

A king sits on his throne to judge. He gets
rid of all evil when he sees it.

PROVERBS 20:8

Princess Thoughts

A leader or king takes time to make good decisions.
A good leader will make decisions that help people.
God always makes good decisions.

A Prayer for the King

Father King, please help our leaders make good decisions.
Help me to make good decisions too.

Princess in Action

When you need to make a choice, sit and think. Ask God to
help you make the right choice. Think about what choice
will help people and what choice might hurt someone. Think
about decisions you make. Screaming and shouting inside is a
bad choice. A good choice is to talk with an inside or quiet
voice when you are indoors.

Princess Thinking

Royal Words

You have been raised up with Christ. So think about things that are in heaven. That is where Christ is. He is sitting at God's right hand.

COLOSSIANS 3:1

Princess Thoughts

Jesus sits on a throne in heaven. If you believe that Jesus died for your sins and have asked Jesus to forgive your sins, you will live forever in heaven. Jesus wants us to remember heaven, because that is where he lives.

A Prayer for the King

Lord Jesus, thanks for reminding me that heaven is a wonderful place.

Princess in Action

Heaven is filled with love. We can share God's love with people every day to let them know God loves them. He wants them in heaven too. Share your toys today as a reminder that God shares heaven with you.

Clear Thinking

Royal Words

The people went out to see what had happened.
Then they came to Jesus. They found the man
who was now free of the demons. He was sitting at
Jesus' feet. He was dressed and thinking clearly.

LUKE 8:35

Princess Thoughts

Jesus healed a man who was acting crazy. His mind was not
working right. The man didn't wear clothes. He lived in a
cemetery. When the man was healed, he sat by Jesus,
all dressed and peaceful.

A Prayer for the King

Lord Jesus, I am happy you can heal people's minds.
Please keep my mind healthy.

Princess in Action

Practice using your mind. If you have a puzzle, put it together.
If you have a matching game, play that
with your mommy or daddy.

Following a Path

Royal Words

You [Lord] always show me the path that leads to
life. You will fill me with joy when I am with you.
Acts 2:28

Princess Thoughts

Paths in the woods are fun to follow. As we grow up, we have
choices to make. Some choices are big ones, like who to marry or
what kind of job to get. We make choices every day. Sometimes
we choose to be good. Sometimes we choose to break a rule.
Good choices keep us on God's path.

A Prayer for the King

Father God, I am happy you show me which way to go. Guide me in life.

Princess in Action

Do a coin-toss walk along a path with your family. Every time
there's a choice of which way to go, stop and thank God for
helping you make good choices in life. Then toss a coin. Go to the
right for heads and left for tails. This is an easy way to choose.
Talk about how God's Word helps us make good choices.

April 27

Show-Off Noses

Royal Words
Don't show it off against me. Don't speak with your noses in the air.
PSALM 75:5

Princess Thoughts
Showing off means to act like you are better than other people because you have something they don't. It's fun to show off new clothes. But it's unkind when a person acts like she is better than other people. Putting your nose in the air means you are stuck up. It means you think you are better than other people. Being stuck up is not kind. It's rude.

A Prayer for the King
Father King, you love everyone so much. Help me to be kind to all the people you made.

Princess in Action
Be polite when you speak to others. Practice saying "please" and "thank you" all day. Smile instead of turning away from someone who wears old clothes or looks dirty.

April 28

Honor Your Parents

Royal Words

Scripture says, "Honor your father and mother."
That is the first commandment that has a promise.
"Then things will go well with you."
EPHESIANS 6:2-3

Princess Thoughts

One of God's rules is to honor your parents. That means God
wants you to listen, obey, and be polite to your mommy and daddy.
This rule comes with a promise that you will have a good life.

A Prayer for the King

Father God, help me to honor my parents.

Princess in Action

Show you honor your parents by obeying them when they ask you
to do something. Pray for them. Do something nice for them like
making their bed or getting them a snack.

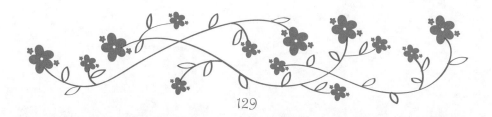

Respect for God

Royal Words

A father is tender and kind to his children.
In the same way, the LORD is tender and kind
to those who have respect for him.

PSALM 103:13

Princess Thoughts

God is a good father. He is kind to us. God wants us to respect him. *Respect* means to have a good attitude toward the person. You show respect to God when you obey God and listen to him.

A Prayer for the King

Father God, you are special. Help me to respect you.

Princess in Action

When you pray, greet God with words like "Father King," "Dear Daddy," or "Lord Almighty." Those words show God is great. Each time you pray, thank God for his love. Thank him for blessings in your life like your family and friends.

April 30

Respect for the Poor

Royal Words

[The Lord] raises poor people up from the trash pile.
He lifts needy people out of the ashes. He lets them
sit with princes. He gives them places of honor.

1 SAMUEL 2:8

Princess Thoughts

God cares about poor people. God likes his followers to share
what they have with the poor. Both rich people and poor
people are important to God.

A Prayer for the King

Father King, thank you for caring for poor people. Please help
me to care for them too.

Princess in Action

If a neighbor doesn't have a job, your family can pray for
your neighbor. Show friends they are important to God
whether they are rich or poor.

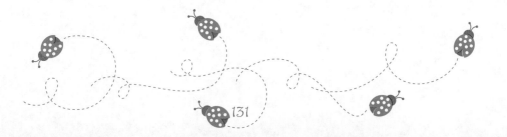

May

Welcoming Jesus

Royal Words

Jesus came to a village where a woman named Martha
lived. She welcomed him into her home.

LUKE 10:38

Princess Thoughts

When Jesus came to town, a woman named Martha welcomed
him into her house. That means Martha invited Jesus to her house
and helped him feel comfortable.

A Prayer for the King

Lord Jesus, how wonderful to know you are with me! I want
you to feel welcomed in my life and my home.

Princess in Action

Imagine if Jesus visited your home. What food would you
serve him? What would you say to him? Well, Jesus is with
you, even if you can't see him. You can start by greeting him
now. You could say, "Hello, Jesus. I'm happy you are here."
Each morning greet Jesus and welcome him to your day.

Sitting with Guests

Royal Words

[Martha] had a sister named Mary. Mary sat at the
Lord's feet listening to what he said. But Martha was
busy with all the things that had to be done.

LUKE 10:39-40

Princess Thoughts

Martha worked while Jesus was visiting. But Mary sat and enjoyed
talking with Jesus. It's not fun to have a friend visit while you pick
up your toys. It's more fun to play and have fun together. Mary sat
and listened to her friend. She enjoyed being with Jesus.

A Prayer for the King

Jesus, King of kings, help me remember to sit and listen when my
parents tell me about you.

Princess in Action

Practice listening. Ask your mom or dad these questions to find
out something new: What is your favorite color?
What is your favorite Bible story?
Listen for your mom's or dad's answers.

Choose Peace

Royal Words

Tell [God's people] not to speak evil things against anyone.
Remind them to live in peace. They must consider the needs
of others. They must be kind and gentle toward all people.

TITUS 3:2

Princess Thoughts

Living in peace is more fun than fighting. Today's Bible verse gives
us three steps to help live in peace. First, don't say bad things
about other people. Second, think of what other people need
instead of what you want. Third, be kind. A kind person is patient
with others and uses good manners.

A Prayer for the King

Father King, help me to be a kind and peaceful person.

Princess in Action

Practice your manners to show kindness.
Learn when to say "Excuse me" and "I'm sorry."
Hold a door open for someone.

Welcoming People

Royal Words

Share with God's people who are in need.
Welcome others into your homes.

ROMANS 12:13

Princess Thoughts

God wants us to welcome people when they visit our homes.
That means we should share our toys and be nice to people
who visit us.

A Prayer for the King

Father God, I am happy I have a home to welcome guests to.
Help me to be kind when people come to visit me.

Princess in Action

With a grown-up's help, practice going to the door and
greeting guests with a smile. If you have a welcome mat at
your door, sweep it to help keep it clean.

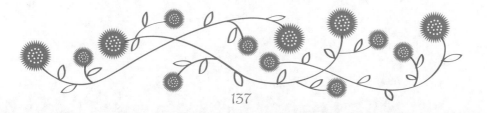

May 5

Wells for Water

Royal Words

God opened Hagar's eyes. She saw a well of water.
So she went and filled the bottle with water.
And she gave the boy a drink.

GENESIS 21:19

Princess Thoughts

Most people turn on a faucet to get water. In the Bible,
people got their water from a well. Hagar thought she and her
little son would die in the desert because there was no water.
But God showed her a well so they could drink. *Gurgle.*
Gurgle. She filled a container and gave her son a drink.
Gulp. Gulp. Fresh water saved them.

A Prayer for the King

Father King, thanks for clean water to drink
and to clean my body and clothes with.

Princess in Action

Enjoy a big glass of water. Many people in poor countries
don't have clean water because they can't dig wells.
Ask your mom or dad if your family can give money
to help dig wells for the poor.

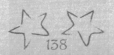

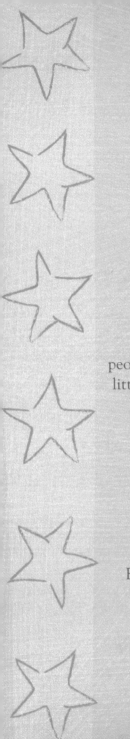

Party Manners

Royal Words

The people of the island were unusually kind. It was raining and cold. So they built a fire and welcomed all of us.

ACTS 28:2

Princess Thoughts

Paul, a follower of Jesus, sailed on a ship with a group of men. But a great storm came and smashed the boat. *Crash! Splash!* The men all swam to an island and lived. Hooray! The people who lived on the island welcomed Paul and the other men and treated them with kindness. They built a fire to warm Paul and the other men who were cold and wet from the storm.

A Prayer for the King

Father King, I am thankful you can save people from bad storms. Help me to be kind, especially when we have unexpected guests.

Princess in Action

Be kind to everyone who visits your home. Sometimes people may surprise you with a visit. Offer them a place to sit. Offer them a snack and a drink.

Jesus Heals a Little Girl

Royal Words

He begged Jesus, "Please come. My little daughter is dying.
Place your hands on her to heal her. Then she will live."

MARK 5:23

Princess Thoughts

A man named Jairus asked Jesus to heal his daughter.
Jairus was polite and said, "Please." Jesus walked with the
man while many people followed. Then he entered the man's
home and healed the little girl.

A Prayer for the King

Lord Jesus, please listen to me and answer my prayers.

Princess in Action

When you speak to Jesus, be polite. Jesus listens to many prayers.
Sit still and wait for one minute. Think of how Jesus sometimes
wants you to wait for him to answer your prayers.

A Filled Cup

Royal Words

You [Lord] prepare a feast for me right in front of my enemies. You pour oil on my head. My cup runs over.

PSALM 23:5

Princess Thoughts

In Bible times, a host would pour oil on his guests' heads to show that he liked them. In this psalm, God is the host. God gives his guest a feast. God anoints the guest with oil that smells good, like perfume. God fills the guest's cup so much that it spills over.

A Prayer for the King

Father King, I am happy you take care of me. Thank you for giving me good things.

Princess in Action

Over the next few days plan a tea party for your princess friends. Talk to your mom about ways you can make each guest feel special at your tea party. Be sure to read tomorrow's devotional for the next step in planning your party.

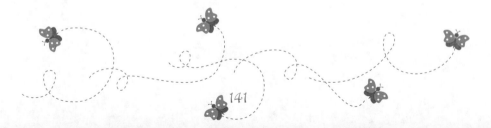

Invitations

Royal Words
Welcome others into your homes
without complaining.
1 Peter 4:9

Princess Thoughts
Jesus wants us to help make everyone feel special by
welcoming them. That means we should greet our guests
with a smile. We should be happy to see them too.

A Prayer for the King
Lord Jesus, help me to welcome people into my home.

Princess in Action
Invite friends to your tea party. Tell your friends
that you really want them to come. Ask them what
games they like to play. Remember to play those
games when they come.

Sweet Treats

Royal Words

[The head waiter] said to [the bridegroom], "Everyone brings out the best wine first. They bring out the cheaper wine after the guests have had too much to drink. But you have saved the best until now."

JOHN 2:10

Princess Thoughts

When the hosts ran out of drinks at the wedding, Jesus turned water into wine. He made a drink that tasted better than what the hosts had bought. The waiter praised the bridegroom for saving the best drinks. The waiter didn't know about the miracle.

A Prayer for the King

Lord Jesus, you care about special parties and people's celebrations. Thank you for loving us so much.

Princess in Action

Plan the food and drinks for your tea party.
Be sure to serve the best food and drinks you can to guests.
That helps them feel special.

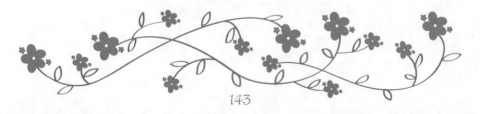

Tea Party Prayers

Royal Words
[The apostles] all came together regularly to pray.
ACTS 1:14

Princess Thoughts
Jesus' followers got together and prayed. People can pray
whenever they are together.

A Prayer for the King
Dear God, I am happy you like people to pray together.
Thank you for listening to our prayers.

Princess in Action
When your friends are with you for your tea party, say a prayer.
Thank God for the food and for your friends.

No Worries

Royal Words

"If that is how God dresses the wild grass, won't he dress you even better? . . . So don't worry. Don't say, 'What will we eat?' Or, 'What will we drink?' Or, 'What will we wear?'"

MATTHEW 6:30-31

Princess Thoughts

Jesus talked to worried people who wondered what they would eat or wear. He told them to trust God and to stop worrying. Jesus pointed to flowers in the grass and reminded the people that the beautiful petals on flowers come from God. God cares for you more than he cares for the flowers.

A Prayer for the King

Father King, thanks for dressing flowers with beautiful petals in all sorts of colors. Help me to trust you instead of worrying.

Princess in Action

Take a family nature walk to see how God dresses up the flowers, trees, and even weeds. Let Mom or Dad take photos of you standing next to pretty flowers.

May 13

A Tea Party with Grandma

Royal Words

Stand up in order to show your respect for old people.
Also have respect for me. I am the LORD your God.

LEVITICUS 19:32

Princess Thoughts

God wants us to be kind and respectful to people who
have lived a long time. Grandmas are much older than
you. They are wise from years of learning. God is even
older and wiser than the oldest, wisest person. Be kind
to older people.

A Prayer for the King

Father King, thank you for giving us grandmas and grandpas.
Help me to be kind to the older people in my life.

Princess in Action

Invite your grandma or another older person to come
to your house for a tea party. Open the door for her,
and serve her the food. Listen to her wise words.
Let someone take a picture of the two of you having tea.

146

Dinner with Jesus

Royal Words

Zacchaeus came down at once and welcomed [Jesus] gladly.

Luke 19:6

Princess Thoughts

Zacchaeus was a short man. He climbed a tree just to look over the people's heads to see Jesus. Jesus saw Zacchaeus, stopped below the tree, and talked to him. This surprised everyone, including Zacchaeus. Jesus ate dinner at the home of his new friend Zacchaeus.

A Prayer for the King

Lord Jesus, I am happy that you see me and want to be with me.

Princess in Action

Jesus wants to be with you. Have a dinner party for Jesus. Set out a plate and cup for him. Talk to Jesus as you enjoy your dinner.

The Cup Jesus Shared

Royal Words

After the supper [Jesus] took the cup. He said, "This cup is
the new covenant in my blood. It is poured out for you."
LUKE 22:20

Princess Thoughts

Jesus used a cup when he had his last supper with his friends. Jesus
gave thanks to God the Father and then held up the cup. He told
his friends that this cup and the bread they ate represented his
death on the cross. Today, people at church remember Jesus' death
on the cross by eating bread and drinking grape juice.
This is called Communion.

A Prayer for the King

Lord Jesus, thank you for giving us Communion to help us
remember that you died for our sins.

Princess in Action

Talk about Communion with your family. What is something your
family could do to remember that Jesus died on the cross for your
sins? When people are having a meal and want to cheer for
someone or something, they hold up their cups and gently tap
their cups together. Tap your glass to your mommy's glass and say,
"Cheers for Jesus" or "Thanks, Jesus, for the Cross."

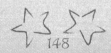

God Listens to His Princess

Royal Words

[The Lord said,] "Now my eyes will see [my people].
My ears will pay attention to the prayers they offer
in this place."

2 CHRONICLES 7:15

Princess Thoughts

God spoke to King Solomon long ago. He told Solomon
that he listens to his people. God pays attention to what
they say, and he sees them as they speak.

A Prayer for the King

Father God, thanks for listening to my prayers
and for watching over me.

Princess in Action

God listens to you, his princess. Draw or write your
prayer requests on a piece of paper. When God answers
a prayer, put a star on the paper. Thank Jesus for the
prayers he has answered.

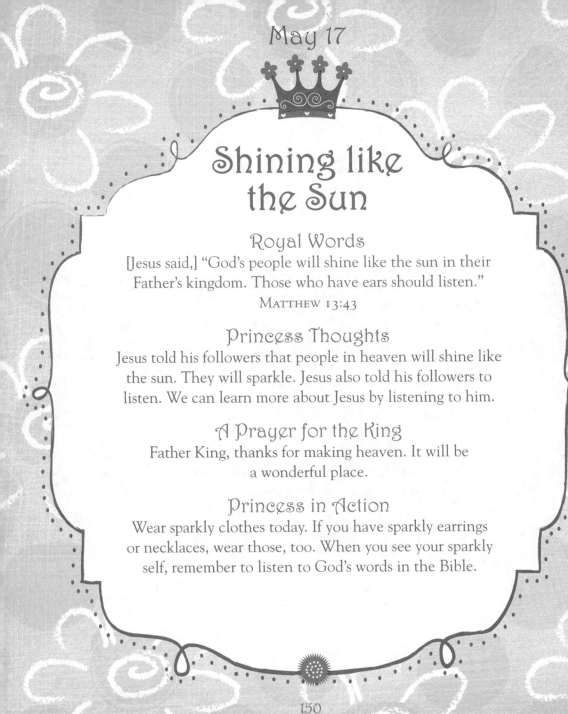

Follow the Right Voice

Royal Words

You will hear your Teacher's voice behind you. You will
hear it whether you turn to the right or the left. It will say,
"Here is the path I want you to take. So walk on it."

ISAIAH 30:21

Princess Thoughts

God is our teacher. God teaches us through the Bible.
As you learn and follow what the Bible says, you will
understand how to make good choices. As you pray,
God will show you what to do.

A Prayer for the King

Father God, help me to listen to your words and to follow you.

Princess in Action

Play hide-and-seek with a twist. Ask someone to hide
and then call out to you. Follow that person's voice
to find him or her.

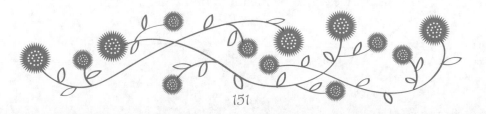

Love Is Polite

Royal Words

[Love] is not rude. It does not look out for its own interests.
It does not easily become angry. It does not
keep track of other people's wrongs.

1 Corinthians 13:5

Princess Thoughts

God loves you, his princess. Many people love you, and you are
learning to love other people. *Love* means to care about other
people and to not be selfish. A selfish person may have a temper
tantrum or yell if she does not get her way. But a caring person
shares and says nice things to other people.

A Prayer for the King

Father King, thanks for loving me. Help me to love other people.
When I feel angry, help me to stop and think about love instead.

Princess in Action

Squirt lemon juice or vinegar on something before you
eat it. Notice how it makes the food taste sour. Saying
mean things makes words sound sour. God doesn't want
his princesses to be mean. When you feel angry,
stop and pray.

When God Whispered

Royal Words

After the earthquake a fire came. But the LORD wasn't in the
fire. And after the fire there was only a gentle whisper.

1 KINGS 19:12

Princess Thoughts

Elijah was a man who believed in God. He listened to hear God
speak. A great wind whipped by that even tore mountains apart.
But God didn't speak in the wind. An earthquake and a fire also
came. But Elijah didn't hear God in those, either. Then Elijah
heard a little whisper. That was God's voice. Sometimes God
whispers to us.

A Prayer for the King

Father God, help me to listen for your voice.
Help me to obey your words.

Princess in Action

You don't need to shout to be heard. Shouting and other loud
noises can be like the wind that broke the mountain. Practice your
indoor voice. Practice whispering.

Jumping for Joy

Royal Words

[Elizabeth said to Mary,] "As soon as I heard the sound of your voice, the baby inside me jumped for joy."

LUKE 1:44

Princess Thoughts

A mother feels her growing baby moving inside her. The baby wiggles, kicks, rolls, and pushes. Elizabeth's baby, John, was inside her. Mary's baby, Jesus, was inside Mary. When Elizabeth heard Mary's voice, Elizabeth's baby, John, jumped for joy.

A Prayer for the King

Father King, let me jump for joy because your Son, Jesus, came.

Princess in Action

Today, every time you hear the name Jesus, jump for joy.

God in Nature

Royal Words

Ever since the world was created, people have seen the earth
and sky. Through everything God made, they can clearly
see his invisible qualities—his eternal power and divine
nature. So they have no excuse for not knowing God.

Romans 1:20, nlt

Princess Thoughts

We may not be able to see God like we can see our friends
and family. But we can see the things God has created.
Every plant and animal is a reminder that God is creative
and that he made the world.

A Prayer for the King

Creator God, you made a beautiful world full of so many animals
and plants. Thank you for making each one different.

Princess in Action

Take an "I spy" walk. Go for a walk with your family. Have your
mom or dad write down the different plants, animals, and birds
that you spy. Thank God for all he made.

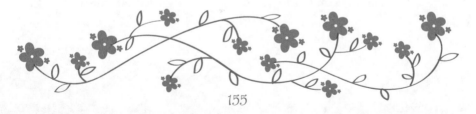

Healing a Deaf Man

Royal Words

Jesus took the man to one side, away from the crowd. He put his fingers into the man's ears. Then he spit and touched the man's tongue. . . . The man's ears were opened. His tongue was freed up, and he began to speak clearly.

MARK 7:33, 35

Princess Thoughts

Jesus healed a man who could not hear or speak. Jesus spit and touched the man's tongue. Many people who cannot hear use sign language. Some deaf people can read lips to understand what people are saying. Doctors are working to find new ways to help deaf people hear.

A Prayer for the King

Father King, thank you for making our ears. Please continue to heal people who can't hear or speak.

Princess in Action

Put your hands on your ears. Ask a parent to whisper something from across the room. Can you hear it? This is what it was like for the deaf man in the Bible before Jesus healed him.

Listen to the Shepherd

Royal Words

[Jesus said,] "My sheep listen to my voice.
I know them, and they follow me."

JOHN 10:27

Princess Thoughts

Jesus is our shepherd. Like sheep follow a shepherd, we can
follow Jesus and learn to hear his voice. Jesus cares for us like
a shepherd cares for his little lambs.

A Prayer for the King

Lord Jesus, thanks for caring for me. Help me
to hear your voice.

Princess in Action

Pray and listen for Jesus. Sometimes he will bring a
verse to your mind. Sometimes he will help you
know how to make the right decision. Share with
someone how God has helped you.

A Heart That Listened

Royal Words

One of those listening was a woman named Lydia.
She was from the city of Thyatira. Her business was
selling purple cloth. She was a worshiper of God. The
Lord opened her heart to accept Paul's message.

Acts 16:14

Princess Thoughts

Lydia worked hard and sold expensive purple cloth to people.
Lydia worshiped God, but she had never heard that Jesus had died
on the cross for her sins. So Paul taught Lydia about Jesus. Lydia
listened and asked Jesus to forgive her sins.

A Prayer for the King

Lord Jesus, thank you for people who teach us about you.
Please help the people I love to believe in you.

Princess in Action

Draw a picture of a heart. Have your mom or dad
write in the names of people you love. Pray that
those people will love Jesus.

May 26

Learning God's Word

Royal Words

Then all of the people went away to eat and drink. They
shared their food with others. They celebrated with great
joy. Now they understood the words they had heard. That's
because everything had been explained to them.

NEHEMIAH 8:12

Princess Thoughts

For a while, God's people forgot to read the Bible. Nehemiah had the
church leaders read the Scripture and explain what the words meant.
The people felt bad and cried because they had not listened to God.
But Nehemiah told them to celebrate and rejoice
because they were listening now.

A Prayer for the King

Father King, thanks for giving us the Bible so we can understand your
ways and your love. Help me to listen to your Word every day.

Princess in Action

Read today's verse again. Talk about what it means. Then have a parent
show you the verse in your Bible, and put a bookmark there. Talk about
how God's words make you happy. Celebrate with a special snack.

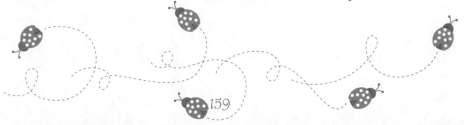

Listen

Royal Words

"Still other seed fell on good soil. It grew up and produced
a crop 100 times more than the farmer planted."
When Jesus said this, he called out, "Those who have
ears should listen."

LUKE 8:8

Princess Thoughts

Jesus wanted the people to pay attention. He told a story about a
farmer who planted seeds. Only the seeds planted in good soil grew
a big crop. God wants people's hearts to be like good soil. He
wants the words in the Bible to change us when we listen to them.

A Prayer for the King

Lord Jesus, help my heart be good soil.

Princess in Action

Go outside and check for good soil. See where plants are growing
well. Let someone read the whole story about the farmer and the
seeds. (It's in Luke 8:4-15.) Listen well. See if you can retell the
story or act it out as a play.

May 28

Listen to Learn

Royal Words

The Lord and King has taught me what to say. He has taught me how to help those who are tired. He wakes me up every morning. He makes me want to listen like a good student.

Isaiah 50:4

Princess Thoughts

You've read God's words in this book for many days. You've been learning how to help other people. It's exciting to hear what the Bible says and to learn how to be a princess. Listening helps you learn.

A Prayer for the King

Father King, thanks for giving me ears to hear. Help me to learn something new every day.

Princess in Action

State one new fact you learned today. Learning helps you grow smarter.

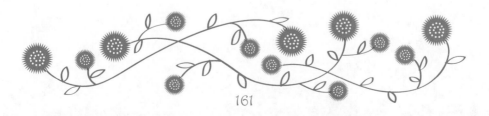

Storytelling

Royal Words
My child, listen and be wise. Keep your
heart on the right path.
PROVERBS 23:19

Princess Thoughts
The book of Proverbs in the Bible contains many
wise sayings. As you listen to the Bible, you'll grow wiser.
God wants you to wisely choose to love him and to
follow him. That's the right path.

A Prayer for the King
Father King, I am thankful you are so wise and teach me
to be wise through the Bible.

Princess in Action
Show your mom or dad that you have listened to the Bible.
Talk about a Bible story you have learned.

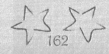

House on a Rock

Royal Words

[Jesus said,] "Some people come to me and listen to me and do what I say. . . . They are like someone who builds a house. He digs down deep and sets it on solid rock. When a flood comes, the river rushes against the house. But the water can't shake it. The house is well built."

LUKE 6:47-48

Princess Thoughts

Jesus told a story about two people who built houses. The person who dug deep and built his house on the rock was wise. He started with a good foundation that would stand firm in most storms. This house took longer to build, but it was a stronger and safer house.

A Prayer for the King

Lord Jesus, help me take my time to do things well.

Princess in Action

Find two rocks. Use chalk to draw a picture on one of the rocks. Ask a parent to use a permanent marker to write your name on the other rock. Run the rocks under water. Which lasts longer—the chalk or the marker?

House on Sand

Royal Words

[Jesus said,] "But everyone who hears these words of mine and does not put them into practice is like a foolish man who built his house on sand. The rain came down, the streams rose, and the winds blew and beat against that house, and it fell with a great crash."

MATTHEW 7:26-27, NIV

Princess Thoughts

One person built his house on a rock. But the other person built his house on sand. Jesus called the person who built a house on sand foolish. That's like building a sand castle that washes away easily. It doesn't take long to build, but the house does not last.

A Prayer for the King

Father King, help me to be patient when things take longer to do.

Princess in Action

Make a sand castle or a dirt cake. Can you draw on it? Pour water on it and watch the sand or dirt float away.

June

The Best Scroll

Royal Words
Be glad that your names are written in heaven.
LUKE 10:20

Princess Thoughts
Jesus gave people the best reason to be happy and rejoice. He said to be happy that your name is written in heaven. Hooray! God writes the names of everyone who believes in him and who will live in heaven one day.

A Prayer for the King
Father King, thank you for writing our names in heaven when we believe in you.

Princess in Action
With a grown-up's help, cut out a crown. Write your name on the crown and decorate it. Your crown is a reminder that God loves you and writes down your name in heaven.

June 2

How Heaven Grows

Royal Words

Jesus told the crowd another story. He said, "The kingdom
of heaven is like a mustard seed. Someone took the seed
and planted it in a field. It is the smallest of all your seeds.
But when it grows, it is the largest of all garden plants. It
becomes a tree. Birds come and rest in its branches."

MATTHEW 13:31-32

Princess Thoughts

Jesus talked about how a tiny seed grows to be a big tree. Just like a
little seed grows, heaven is growing too. Heaven grows when more
people believe in Jesus.

A Prayer for the King

Lord Jesus, I am happy that heaven keeps growing and that there
is room for everyone.

Princess in Action

Write names or draw pictures of people, like people in the Bible,
who are in heaven.

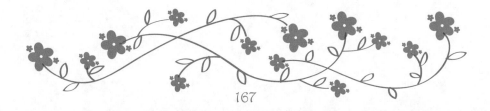

June 3

Blessed Children

Royal Words

[Jesus] took the children in his arms. He put
his hands on them and blessed them.

MARK 10:16

Princess Thoughts

Jesus loves children. He blesses them in the Bible. He
loves you and wants to bless you, his princess. A blessing
shows you are special to Jesus.

A Prayer for the King

Lord Jesus, thanks for loving me and blessing me.

Princess in Action

Have a grown-up write Numbers 6:24 on a piece of
paper: "May the LORD bless you and take good care of
you." Decorate the paper. Put it where you can see it as a
reminder that you are special to Jesus.

June 4

Blessed Home

Royal Words

[David said,] "Now please bless my royal house."
2 SAMUEL 7:29

Princess Thoughts

David lived in a palace because he was a king. David asked God to bless his house. King David wanted God to bless the people who lived there and all who would live there in the future.

A Prayer for the King

Father King, bless my home and my family. Help us to share your love in our house.

Princess in Action

Walk through your home and pray in each room, asking God to bless your house. Ask God to bless the people who live in your home and people who visit.

June 5

Showers of Blessings

Royal Words

[The Lord said,] "I will bless them. I will also bless the places surrounding my holy mountain of Zion. I will send down rain at the right time. There will be showers of blessing."

Ezekiel 34:26

Princess Thoughts

God told his people that he would bless them. The people needed rain to grow food, and God promised to send showers as one blessing. That meant the people would have a good crop and plenty of food.

A Prayer for the King

Lord, thanks for the rain that waters the plants and trees. Thanks for all your blessings.

Princess in Action

Use a hose or watering can to shower some plants. Watch the water drop on leaves and run into the dirt to water the plants.

Blessed Princess

Royal Words

Isaac had faith. So he blessed Jacob and Esau.
He told them what was ahead for them.

HEBREWS 11:20

Princess Thoughts

Isaac blessed his two sons. His blessing celebrated that Jacob
and Esau were children of God. He asked God to care for his
children's future. God told Isaac about his sons' futures, and
then Isaac told his sons what God said.

A Prayer for the King

Father King, I am blessed to be your princess. I know you
have good plans for my future.

Princess in Action

Let your mom and dad bless you. They can write a blessing on
a letter to state their love and their prayer for your future.
Keep the letter in a special place.

A Little Faith and a Great Blessing

Royal Words

[Jesus] replied, "Because your faith is much too small. What I'm about to tell you is true. If you have faith as small as a mustard seed, it is enough. You can say to this mountain, 'Move from here to there.' And it will move. Nothing will be impossible for you."

MATTHEW 17:20

Princess Thoughts

A mustard seed is very tiny. Jesus said even a little tiny faith brings big results. So believe when you pray, because nothing is impossible. You are blessed to have faith.

A Prayer for the King

Lord Jesus, help me to believe you will answer my prayers.

Princess in Action

Walk to a high place and pray with your family. Look around and see the big world God made. God, who made so much, can answer your prayer, no matter how big it seems.

Naming Blessings

Royal Words
We have all received one blessing after another.
JOHN 1:16

Princess Thoughts
God gives us so much. He gives us food, good health, a place to live, a family, and much more. Each one of those things is a blessing.

A Prayer for the King
Father King, thanks for all my blessings.

Princess in Action
Draw pictures of all your blessings. Make the papers into a book. Thank God for each blessing, and keep this as your blessings book.

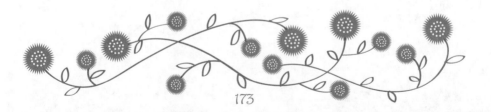

Special Names

Royal Words

[Jacob and Rachel] had a son. . . . [Rachel] continued, "May the LORD give me another son." So she named him Joseph.

GENESIS 30:23-24

Princess Thoughts

Jacob had twelve sons and one daughter. His children's names all meant something. The name Joseph means "increaser" and the name of another son, Judah, means "let God be praised." Your name means something special too.

A Prayer for the King

Father King, thanks for the name my parents gave me. Thanks for my parents.

Princess in Action

Ask your parents how they chose your name, and find out what it means. Make a sign with your name to hang in your room. Ask your mom or dad to write the meaning of your name on the sign. Add glitter and sparkles to make it a princess sign.

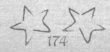

June 10

Strong Arms

Royal Words

She gets ready to work hard. Her arms are strong.
PROVERBS 31:17

Princess Thoughts

Proverbs is a book in the Bible that helps us know how to be wise. One of the proverbs talks about a wonderful woman who is a mother and wife. She works hard, cares for her family, earns money, and cares for the poor. She is a princess with strong muscles. A princess is sweet, but she should also be strong.

A Prayer for the King

Creator God, thanks for making me a girl. Help me to be strong and to help other people.

Princess in Action

Be a strong princess. Exercise your arms to build muscles. You can use a can of food or bottle of water as a weight. Lift it up and down to build muscles. You can use your muscles to help your mom carry laundry or groceries.

Better Than Big Muscles

Royal Words
I can do everything by the power of
Christ. He gives me strength.
PHILIPPIANS 4:13

Princess Thoughts
Jesus has more power than any person on the earth. People
can do great things with the help of Jesus. He helps people
when they think they need more strength or energy.

A Prayer for the King
Lord Jesus, thank you for helping me do great things.

Princess in Action
Try lifting something heavy. Now try lifting it with
someone's help. There are more muscles to share the
work when someone else helps. Christ wants to help you
too. Think of something you are learning to do now,
and pray for Christ to help you.

Muscle Food

Royal Words

Give me some raisins to make me strong. Give me
some apples to make me feel like new again.
Song of Songs 2:5

Princess Thoughts

Good food helps build strong muscles and keeps you healthy.
Raisins contain iron that makes the blood strong. Apples contain
natural sugar that gives energy to your body. The nutrients in
apples help you remember what you're learning.

A Prayer for the King

Father King, thanks for making healthy fruits, like apples.
Thank you for grapes that are dried to make raisins.

Princess in Action

Make a snack of apples and raisins or another healthy treat.
Share the snack with your family.

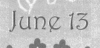

Awesome God

Royal Words

[God is] the only one who can spread the heavens out.
He alone can walk on the waves of the ocean.

JOB 9:8

Princess Thoughts

God is so fabulous. He is King of everything, and you are his
princess. God made the heavens. Wow! He can walk on
waves in the ocean too.

A Prayer for the King

Dear Lord, thanks for making waves in the ocean.
You are an awesome God!

Princess in Action

God can walk on water, but we can't. Talk to your mom or dad
about ways you can stay safe in the water.

June 14

Swift Runners

Royal Words

In a race all the runners run. But only one gets the prize. You know that, don't you? So run in a way that will get you the prize.

1 CORINTHIANS 9:24

Princess Thoughts

Zoom! The runner who finishes first wins the race. You get faster with practice. The winner may be the fastest runner. Or the winner may be a slower runner who keeps following the path and finishes.

A Prayer for the King

Father King, thank you for leg muscles that help me run fast. Thank you that I can learn your Word and do what it says.

Princess in Action

Ask an adult to time you as you run to a finish line. You can decide on a spot for the finish line. Find out your time. Try to run faster the next time.

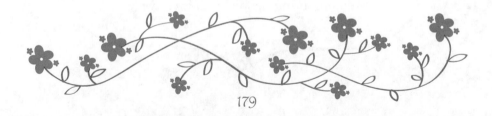

A Strong Heart

Royal Words

I want their hearts to be made cheerful and strong.
I want them to be joined together in love. Then their
understanding will be rich and complete. They will
know the mystery of God. That mystery is Christ.

COLOSSIANS 2:2

Princess Thoughts

Your heart is a muscle, so exercise makes it stronger. God wants
your heart to be healthy and filled with love. This verse reminds
us that other Christians encourage us. They help us understand
God's Word to make our hearts happy.

A Prayer for the King

Father God, thanks for giving me a heart that beats strong.
Help me to love others.

Princess in Action

Exercising can keep your heart muscle strong and
healthy. Run around, dance, or do jumping jacks. When
you're done exercising, make your heart cheerful by
remembering people who love you.

June 16

A Rich Heart

Royal Words
Your heart will be where your riches are.
Matthew 6:21

Princess Thoughts
Jesus talked about treasure, but he didn't mean gold, silver, and jewels. He talked about a different treasure. Jesus saw that people cared more about things like toys, money, and clothes. He wants us to treasure him and people.

A Prayer for the King
Father King, I'm happy you love and treasure me. Help me to care more about people than things.

Princess in Action
Cut out a big heart. Draw or glue on pictures of people you treasure. Hang it up, and remember to care more for people than toys or money.

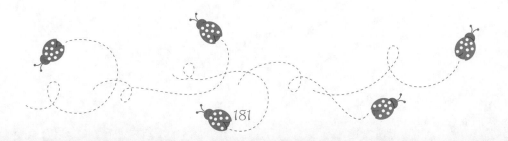

Treasuring God's Word

Royal Words

Let Christ's word live in you like a rich treasure. Teach
and correct each other wisely. Sing psalms, hymns and
spiritual songs. Sing with thanks in your hearts to God.

COLOSSIANS 3:16

Princess Thoughts

God's words are treasures. God wants us to share his words.
God also wants us to sing songs that praise him and to be
thankful when we sing.

A Prayer for the King

Dear Father, I thank you for songs and for your love.

Princess in Action

Write or draw a picture about your favorite verse.
Put it in a box to start collecting favorite verses you
learn. This is your treasure box of verses.

God Treasures You

Royal Words

[The Lord said,] "Obey me completely. Keep my covenant.
If you do, then out of all of the nations you will be
my special treasure. The whole earth is mine."
Exodus 19:5

Princess Thoughts

God wants to treasure you. He asks you to do one thing:
obey his rules.

A Prayer for the King

Father King, help me to obey you. I am happy
that you treasure me.

Princess in Action

God's two big rules are to love him and to love other people.
Show love to someone today. Then put a star or gold sticker
on the Bible verse treasure box you made
for yesterday's devotion. The gold is
a reminder that God treasures you.

June 19

Jesus Is Baptized

Royal Words

When all the people were being baptized, Jesus was baptized
too. And as he was praying, heaven was opened.

LUKE 3:21

Princess Thoughts

Splash! Jesus walked into the river, and his cousin John
baptized him. Heaven opened up when John baptized
Jesus. This was the beginning of Jesus' special work for
people. John baptized people with water as a sign that
God forgave them and washed their sins away.

A Prayer for the King

Dear Lord God, thank you for giving us baptism.

Princess in Action

Talk with your mom and dad about baptism in your
church. Look at photos of baptisms. Water reminds us
that God can wash away our sins on the inside.
Wash your hands, and talk about being clean inside and
out.

God the Father Loves His Son

Royal Words

The Holy Spirit came down on [Jesus] in the form of a
dove. A voice came from heaven. It said, "You are my
Son, and I love you. I am very pleased with you."

LUKE 3:22

Princess Thoughts

Today's verse is about God the Father, God the Son, and God the
Holy Spirit being together. Hooray! When Jesus was baptized, God
the Father spoke from heaven to say that he loves his Son Jesus
and that he is pleased with him. God the Holy Spirit flew down
in the form of a dove and landed on Jesus.

A Prayer for the King

Father King, it is wonderful that you, Jesus, and the Holy
Spirit are one God and work together in love.

Princess in Action

Praise Jesus. Use words like, "Jesus, you are God,"
"You are wonderful," and "I love you, Jesus."

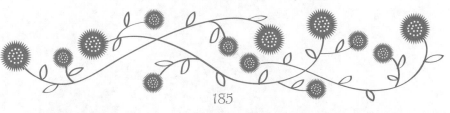

Baby Book

Royal Words

[Joseph] went there with Mary to be listed. Mary was
engaged to him. She was expecting a baby.

LUKE 2:5

Princess Thoughts

All babies are special. But Mary's baby was extra special.
Mary was the mother of Jesus.

A Prayer for the King

Dear Father King, thank you for sending Jesus and
choosing Mary to be his mommy.

Princess in Action

Look at your baby book or photo album filled with your
pictures. That's a book about you. The Bible is a very
special book about God. Parts of it tell about the birth
of God's Son, Jesus.

June 22

Helpful Lights

Royal Words
Your father's commands are like a lamp. Your mother's teaching is like a light. And the training that corrects you leads to life.
PROVERBS 6:23

Princess Thoughts
A good rule helps you do the right thing and keeps you safe. Rules are like a flashlight in the dark that helps you follow a path. Obeying the rules will keep you safe. Following God's rules leads to a good life.

A Prayer for the King
Father God, thanks for light that helps me see in the dark. Help me to follow rules.

Princess in Action
Without light it is hard to follow a path. Set up a path with objects in it. This is an obstacle course. Now let a grown-up blindfold you. Try to walk the path. The grown-up can talk and try to tell you how to get around the objects. When you are done, take off the blindfold and walk the path again.

Good for the Heart

Royal Words

Here is what I want you to know in your hearts. The LORD
your God trains you, just as parents train their children.
DEUTERONOMY 8:5

Princess Thoughts

Moms and dads show their children how to do things like picking
up toys, cooking a meal, and making the bed. That's part of
training you. God trains you too. His words in the Bible tell you
how to be kind to others and how to love God.

A Prayer for the King

Father King, you are wise and want to teach me good skills.
Please help me to listen.

Princess in Action

Obey your parents and God. Put a piece of paper on your
refrigerator, and add stars when you obey. See how fast
you can fill the paper with stars.

June 24

Music for God

Royal Words
All of them were trained and skilled
in playing music for the Lord.
1 Chronicles 25:7

Princess Thoughts
Many people in the Bible learned to play music and sing songs to
praise God. It takes practice to play an instrument or sing well.
God likes when we play music and sing to praise him.

A Prayer for the King
Dear Lord, I thank you for music and songs. Help me
to practice using music to praise you.

Princess in Action
Practice music and dance. Make up your own words
to sing and to praise God with.

Patterns

Royal Words

He is trained to work with gold, silver, bronze and iron.
He knows how to work with stone and wood. He can also
work with purple, blue and bright red yarn and fine linen.
He's skilled in all kinds of carving. He can follow any pattern
you give him. He'll work with your skilled workers.

2 Chronicles 2:14

Princess Thoughts

The workers who built God's Temple knew many skills.
They used their talent to make a beautiful home for God.
The workers understood how to follow directions and
patterns. A pattern is a design that repeats.

A Prayer for the King

Father King, I am happy we have a pretty church to go to.
Help me to learn to make beautiful things.

Princess in Action

Find patterns around your home. You will see them
in clothes, on plates, and even on toys. The next
time you're at church, look for patterns on the
floor, on the ceiling, or on the walls.

Good and Evil

Royal Words

Solid food is for those who are grown up. They have
trained themselves with a lot of practice. They can
tell the difference between good and evil.

HEBREWS 5:14

Princess Thoughts

Grown-ups know a lot. They understand how to be safe.
They know the difference between right and wrong. It's good
to learn those things. It is good to listen to grown-ups
when they teach us.

A Prayer for the King

Father King, help me make good choices. Help me
to know what is good and what is wrong.

Princess in Action

Play a good-and-evil game. Let someone state a choice, like
"sneaking a cookie or waiting for Mommy to give you a cookie."
Tell which choice is good.

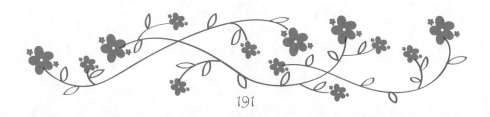

Lights in the Sky

Royal Words

God put the lights in the huge space of the
sky to give light on the earth.

GENESIS 1:17

Princess Thoughts

God wanted us to see the world he made.
He made lights to help us see.

A Prayer for the King

Creator God, thanks for making light
so I can see what is around me.

Princess in Action

Before you go to sleep tonight, use a flashlight to shine into the
corners of your room. What might look scary in the dark
may be a stuffed animal or a toy.

June 28

Guiding Light

Royal Words

Your word is like a lamp that shows me the
way. It is like a light that guides me.

PSALM 119:105

Princess Thoughts

A flashlight or lantern is a lamp that guides the way
when you carry it. In the dark you might stumble over a
rock or walk into a bush. The light helps you see where
to step. The Bible is like a light. It shows you where to
go as you follow God.

A Prayer for the King

Father God, thank you for electricity, batteries,
and other power that makes lights work.

Princess in Action

Take the batteries out of a flashlight. Now turn the flashlight
on. What happens? Put the batteries back in the flashlight
and see it turn on. God's Word gives us power, just like
batteries give power to the flashlight.

Be a Light

Royal Words
You are the light of the world. A city
on a hill can't be hidden.
MATTHEW 5:14

Princess Thoughts
You don't light up like the sun, the stars, or a
lightbulb. But God calls you a light because you can
bring the light of his Word to people. You can share
the Bible to light up people's minds.

A Prayer for the King
Father God, let me shine for you and bring light
to others.

Princess in Action
Let your smile brighten other people's lives. If your
mommy lets you, wear some lip gloss to make your
lips shine. Try to smile at everyone you see today.
Tell some people today's verse.

Jesus Glows

Royal Words

There in front of them [Jesus'] appearance
was changed. His face shone like the sun. His
clothes became as white as the light.

MATTHEW 17:2

Princess Thoughts

Close friends of Jesus climbed up a mountain with him.
When they got to the top, Jesus' friends looked and saw
Jesus glow. His clothes became as bright as light. The
light of heaven was shining down on Jesus.

A Prayer for the King

Lord Jesus, help me to sparkle and look bright when
people see me.

Princess in Action

Get your toys or clothes that glow in the dark. Look
at how bright they glow in the dark, and think
about Jesus looking bright.

July

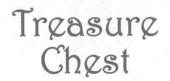

Treasure Chest

Royal Words

[Jesus said,] "Store up for yourselves treasures in heaven, where moths and vermin do not destroy, and where thieves do not break in and steal."

MATTHEW 6:20, NIV

Princess Thoughts

Jesus told people not to worry about keeping treasures like toys or money on earth. He wants us to store up treasures like love in heaven. God places treasures in heaven for us when we show love and give what we have to others.

A Prayer for the King

Father King, thanks for saving treasures in heaven for me.

Princess in Action

Decorate a shoe box to hold special reminders of treasures in heaven. This is your princess treasure chest. Put a paper heart inside the chest as a reminder to treasure love. You will be adding to this treasure chest in devotions to come.

Treasures God Made

Royal Words

You will enjoy the many good things your ships bring you.
You will enjoy treasures that are hidden in the sand.

DEUTERONOMY 33:19

Princess Thoughts

Digging in the sand at the beach for shells and other treasures can
be fun. Sand is a treasure itself. Sand is used to make many things.
Sand is used to make glass and cement. God spoke the words in
today's verse to people who lived near the seashore. Ships
delivered food and other things to the people.

A Prayer for the King

Father King, even the sand you created is amazing. Help me
to enjoy the treasures of the world you made.

Princess in Action

Have fun digging in sand at a playground or finding shells at the
beach. Fill a tiny container with sand. Put it in the princess
treasure chest you made in yesterday's devotion as a reminder
to thank God for all the treasures he created.

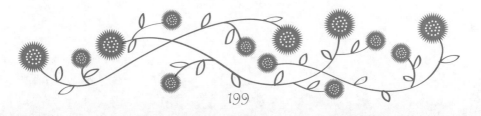

Fun in the Sun

Royal Words

Light is sweet, and it pleases the eyes to see the sun.
ECCLESIASTES 11:7, NIV

Princess Thoughts

God hung the sun in the sky. It's fun to enjoy sunshine
and summer days.

A Prayer for the King

Dear Lord God, thanks for the sun and blue skies.

Princess in Action

Enjoy playing outside. See if the sun is out, if it's hidden by
clouds, or if it's playing peekaboo in the clouds. Stand in
sunshine if it is sunny. Let the sun warm your skin.

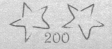

Real Freedom

Royal Words

[Jesus said,] "You will know the truth.
And the truth will set you free."

JOHN 8:32

Princess Thoughts

Today is a day to celebrate freedom in the United States.
People in the United States are free to pray and worship
God. Jesus told us that knowing the truth will give us
freedom. It is good to know what truth is. It is better to
tell the truth than to lie.

A Prayer for the King

Father King, help me to tell the truth. Help people
everywhere be free to worship you.

Princess in Action

Put a little American flag in the princess treasure chest
you made on July 1 as a reminder of freedom.

Gardening

Royal Words
[King Solomon] made gardens and parks and
planted all kinds of fruit trees in them.
ECCLESIASTES 2:5, NIV

Princess Thoughts
King Solomon cared about the earth God made. He made
parks for people to relax in. He planted all kinds of fruit trees.
Fruits that grow where King Solomon lived include bananas,
apricots, figs, pomegranates, dates, pears, and lemons.

A Prayer for the King
Father God, thank you for parks where I can run and play.
Thank you for fruits that taste sweet and help me grow.

Princess in Action
Play at a park, or visit an orchard with fruit trees. Look at the
trees that grow, and thank God for making trees.

Skin Care

Royal Words

[A man] had a skin disease all over his body. . . . He begged [Jesus],
"Lord, if you are willing to make me 'clean,' you can do it."
Jesus reached out his hand and touched the man. "I am willing to
do it," he said. "Be 'clean'!" Right away the disease left him.

LUKE 5:12-13

Princess Thoughts

Jesus met a man with sores on his body. The man asked
Jesus if he would heal him. Jesus said, "I am willing."
Jesus touched the man. In an instant all the man's sores
disappeared. God can heal us, too.

A Prayer for the King

Father King, thanks for healing us when we are sick.
Please keep me healthy.

Princess in Action

Care for your skin, especially on sunny days. Before you
go outside today, put on sunscreen to keep your skin
from getting burned.

July 7

Picnic Fun

Royal Words
When [the disciples] landed, they saw
a fire of burning coals. There were fish
on it. There was also some bread.

JOHN 21:9

Princess Thoughts
After Jesus rose from the dead, he enjoyed a picnic at the
beach with his friends. His friends came in from fishing and
saw that Jesus had cooked fish and bread on a fire.

A Prayer for the King
Lord Jesus, thanks for beaches, cookouts, and friends.

Princess in Action
Make plans for a picnic. Enjoy eating outside and having
fun with your family or friends.

July 8

Swimming

Royal Words

The disciple Jesus loved said to Simon Peter, "It is the Lord!"
As soon as Peter heard that, he put his coat on. He had taken it
off earlier. Then he jumped into the water.

John 21:7

Princess Thoughts

Wow! Peter was excited when he heard that Jesus was on the
sandy shore. Peter jumped in the water and swam to the beach
to be with Jesus.

A Prayer for the King

Father King, thanks for giving us water to swim in.

Princess in Action

Splash around in a pool, or run through a sprinkler. Yell,
"Thank you for the water, Jesus!" as you splash or run around.

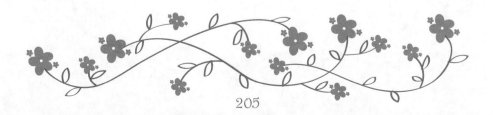

Pure and Holy

Royal Words

God chose us to live pure lives. He wants us to be holy.

1 THESSALONIANS 4:7

Princess Thoughts

Pure means to be without sin. *Holy* means to be like Jesus. We're not perfect. We don't always make the right choice. When we do something wrong and ask for forgiveness, God forgives us. God wants us to choose what is holy and pure.

A Prayer for the King

Lord Jesus, you are perfect, pure, and holy. Help me to follow you. Help me choose to be pure.

Princess in Action

Fill a cup with water. Add objects like paper clips, pebbles, or beads. Chat about how the water is not pure. Use a strainer to remove the objects from the water. Talk about how the strainer helped clean the water. When God forgives us, he removes our sins to make us pure.

Pure Body

Royal Words

How can a young person keep his life pure? By
living in keeping with your word.
PSALM 119:9

Princess Thoughts

It sounds hard to be pure and always make the choice God wants
us to make. God tells us we can be pure by living by the words in
the Bible. That begins by reading and learning what is in the Bible
and making good choices each day.

A Prayer for the King

Father King, you are so wise, and you teach me to be pure through
your words. Help me to remember them and follow them.

Princess in Action

Reading the Bible will help you to make good choices.
Look in your treasure box of verses from the June 17 devotion,
and read the verses you've placed in there. Do you have any more
verses you'd like to add to the box?

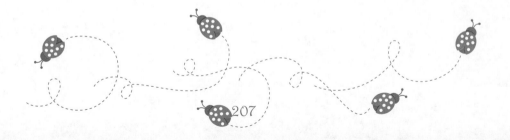

A Different Kind of Body

Royal Words
You are the body of Christ. Each one of you is a part of it.
1 CORINTHIANS 12:27

Princess Thoughts
Another name for the group of Christians around the world is the body of Christ. Each Christian is an important part of the body of Christ. God cares for every person who follows him.

A Prayer for the King
Father King, thanks for caring for everyone who follows you. Help me to remember each Christian is part of the body of Christ.

Princess in Action
Remember that believers should stick together.
Give stickers to your friends who believe in Jesus.

One Body

Royal Words

We are many persons. But in Christ we are one body.
And each part of the body belongs to all the other parts.
ROMANS 12:5

Princess Thoughts

It's good to belong and feel loved. Every Christian
belongs to the body of Christ. We can use our talents
to help other Christians.

A Prayer for the King

Lord Jesus, thanks for loving everyone in your family.
Help me to know how I can help other Christians.

Princess in Action

Find out what different people do at church. Some clean,
some preach sermons, some teach Sunday school, some watch
babies, and some take care of the mail. Make thank-you cards
for church volunteers.

Go in Peace

Royal Words

God is the God who gives peace. May he make you
holy through and through. May your whole spirit, soul
and body be kept free from blame. May you be without
blame from now until our Lord Jesus Christ comes.

1 THESSALONIANS 5:23

Princess Thoughts

God gives us peace and helps us to love one another.
God wants people to be free from doing bad things. God
loves us and forgives us when we do something bad.
God's forgiveness gives us peace.

A Prayer for the King

Lord Jesus, forgive me when I make a bad choice or hurt someone.
Help me to have peace and to feel good inside and out.

Princess in Action

Live in peace. If someone has hurt you, forgive that person today.
Ask God to forgive you for bad things you did.

July 14

You Don't Have to Worry

Royal Words

I tell you, do not worry. Don't worry about your life and what
you will eat or drink. And don't worry about your body and
what you will wear. Isn't there more to life than eating? Aren't
there more important things for the body than clothes?

MATTHEW 6:25

Princess Thoughts

God cares about what we need. He gives us food and homes. We don't
have to worry about having food to eat or clothes to wear. God will give
you just what you need. Be thankful for the blessings God gives you.

A Prayer for the King

Father King, thank you for providing parents, clothes,
a home, and food.

Princess in Action

Write down the things you are thankful for. Go find your favorite toy
and thank God for giving it to you. When you see something you want
at a store or on TV, stop and think about why you want it.
Think about why you don't need it right now.

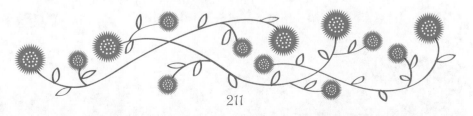

God Knows Your Thoughts

Royal Words

You [Lord] know when I sit down and when I get up.
You know what I'm thinking even though you are far away.
PSALM 139:2

Princess Thoughts

Are you angry, happy, sad, or bored? God knows what
you are thinking. That means he knows how you feel,
too. He hears what you say. He also sees everything you
do. He notices your smiles and tears. He sees when you
help at home.

A Prayer for the King

Father King, I am thankful you can watch me and care
for me. Thank you for paying attention to all my
thoughts and for knowing how I feel.

Princess in Action

Stop and smile at God as you make your bed or pick up
your toys. Thank him for watching over you and
listening to your thoughts.

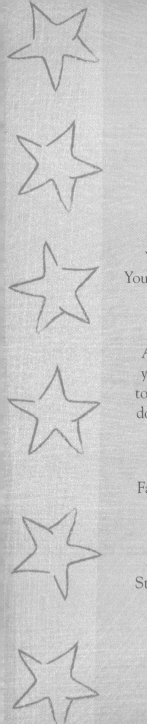

July 16

Animal Lessons

Royal Words

[Ants] aren't very strong. But they store
up their food in the summer.

PROVERBS 30:25

Princess Thoughts

We can watch what God's creatures do and learn from them.
Ants work hard to carry food and store it. Ants are tiny, but
they can carry things that weigh more than they weigh.

A Prayer for the King

Dear God, help me to learn from the creatures you made.

Princess in Action

Grab a magnifying glass and go for an ant walk. When you
find an ant, watch how it works. Work hard, like an ant.

July 17

Cheerful Looks

Royal Words
A cheerful look brings joy to your heart. And good news gives health to your body.

PROVERBS 15:30

Princess Thoughts
A smile and good news makes people feel good. Feeling happy also helps a person stay healthy.

A Prayer for the King
Father King, thank you for the good news that heaven is real. Help me to smile and bring cheer to other people.

Princess in Action
Share smiles with everyone you see today. Tell people that Jesus loves them.

July 18

All Things Are Possible

Royal Words

Jesus looked at them and said, "With man, that is impossible. But with God, all things are possible."

MATTHEW 19:26

Princess Thoughts

There are some things that we can't do. We can't grow wings and fly through the air. We can't leap over tall buildings. We can't tell the sun to shine. But God can do anything. Nothing is impossible for God.

A Prayer for the King

Father King, I am happy you are so great and that nothing is impossible for you. Listen to my prayers, and help me have faith that you will answer them.

Princess in Action

Write or draw your prayer request. Stick it to the refrigerator with a magnet. Look at it and believe God can do anything for you, his princess.

Sharing Treasures

Royal Words

[Jesus] said to them, "Every teacher of the law who has been taught about the kingdom of heaven is like the owner of a house. He brings new treasures out of his storeroom as well as old ones."

MATTHEW 13:52

Princess Thoughts

It's fun to visit a friend who has wonderful toys that she shares with you. Your friend's toys are treasures she takes out from her toy box, shelves, or closet. Jesus said that people who teach about God and his rules are like a friend who shares her great treasures.

A Prayer for the King

Lord Jesus, thank you for my parents and others who teach me about you.

Princess in Action

Celebrate the toys you treasure. Use favorite toys to make a centerpiece for a table. Write and add favorite Bible verses to the table to celebrate the treasure of God's Word.

Sweet Words

Royal Words

Pleasant words are like honey. They are sweet to
the spirit and bring healing to the body.
PROVERBS 16:24

Princess Thoughts

Words make a difference. Words like "please," "I love you," and
"You are doing a great job" make a person feel good. When we feel
good inside, it's easier to get better when we are sick.

A Prayer for the King

Father King, your words are pleasant. Help me to speak kind
and pleasant words.

Princess in Action

Taste a breath mint. It's sweet and makes your breath smell good.
Nice words are like breath mints. Pass out pleasant words. Some
pleasant words are compliments, like "You look pretty." Some
words encourage a person. You can cheer on a friend or brother
or sister when you say, "You can do it!"

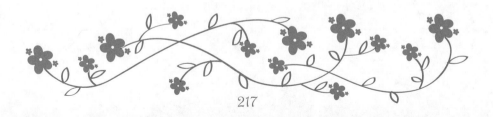

Treasured Memories

Royal Words

Mary kept all these things like a secret treasure in her
heart. She thought about them over and over.

LUKE 2:19

Princess Thoughts

Mary remembered the angels and shepherds who came
to see baby Jesus. She kept these good memories in her
heart and thought about them many times.

A Prayer for the King

Father God, thanks for giving me a mind that remembers things.
Help me to store good memories in my heart.

Princess in Action

Talk about an event you remember. Draw a picture
of it. Place the picture in the princess treasure chest
you made on July 1. Thank God for happy
memories and a mind that can remember.

July 22

Good News

Royal Words

Treasure is kept in clay jars. In the same way, we have the treasure of the good news in these earthly bodies of ours. That shows that the mighty power of the good news comes from God. It doesn't come from us.

2 CORINTHIANS 4:7

Princess Thoughts

A treasure chest holds something valuable, like jewels and money. Our bodies are like treasure chests. The valuable treasures that are inside us are God's love and the truth that Jesus died for us.

A Prayer for the King

Father King, thank you for the good news about Jesus! It is a treasure.

Princess in Action

Your body is a treasure chest. Decorate yourself with pretty clothes and jewelry to remember you hold treasure! Wear a cross or other symbol of Jesus to remember the treasure inside you.

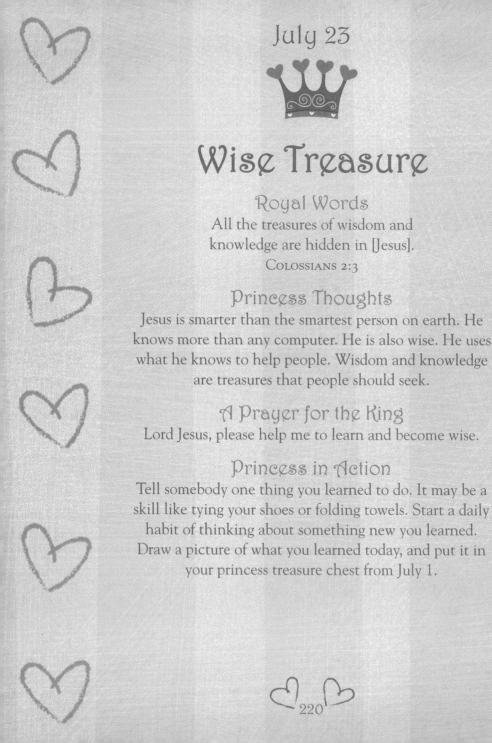

Wise Treasure

Royal Words
All the treasures of wisdom and
knowledge are hidden in [Jesus].
COLOSSIANS 2:3

Princess Thoughts
Jesus is smarter than the smartest person on earth. He
knows more than any computer. He is also wise. He uses
what he knows to help people. Wisdom and knowledge
are treasures that people should seek.

A Prayer for the King
Lord Jesus, please help me to learn and become wise.

Princess in Action
Tell somebody one thing you learned to do. It may be a
skill like tying your shoes or folding towels. Start a daily
habit of thinking about something new you learned.
Draw a picture of what you learned today, and put it in
your princess treasure chest from July 1.

A Good Leader

Royal Words

[The church leader] must welcome people into his home. He must love what is good. He must control his mind and feelings. He must do what is right. He must be holy. He must control what his body longs for.

Titus 1:8

Princess Thoughts

The words in today's verse are part of a list of how church leaders should behave. Church leaders are pastors, Sunday school teachers, and Bible study leaders. It's a great list for everyone to follow. To control your desires means to stop wanting everything you see and to not whine when you don't get your way.

A Prayer for the King

Father God, I have so much. Help me be thankful for what I have instead of wanting more. Help me learn to be a leader at church.

Princess in Action

Ask your mom or dad to write down the names of your pastor, Sunday school teacher, and other leaders at your church. Then pray for each of them. Follow the example of good leaders.

Body by God

Royal Words

[Lord,] your eyes saw my body even before it was formed. You planned how many days I would live. You wrote down the number of them in your book before I had lived through even one of them.

PSALM 139:16

Princess Thoughts

Your mom felt you kick and wiggle inside her, but God saw you first. As God made you, he looked at you and made plans for your life. He knows everything about you and your body. He loves you just the way he made you.

A Prayer for the King

Father King, thanks for giving me a body that moves and grows.

Princess in Action

Look at your baby pictures and see how your body has changed. Put a baby picture in your princess treasure chest that you made on July 1. This picture can be a reminder that God treasures you and made your body so it can move.

July 26

Jesus Heals

Royal Words

News about [Jesus] spread all over Syria. People brought to him all
who were ill with different kinds of sicknesses. Some were suffering
great pain. Others were controlled by demons. Some were shaking
wildly. Others couldn't move at all. And Jesus healed all of them.

MATTHEW 4:24

Princess Thoughts

Jesus saw people who could hardly move, like some people
who are in wheelchairs. He saw people in pain. He helped
the people who couldn't move walk again. He helped sick
people feel better. Jesus can do anything.

A Prayer for the King

Lord Jesus, I am happy that you have the power to heal people.
Please heal people in my church and in my family.

Princess in Action

Wiggle your toes and fingers. Bend over and stand up. Use
your body to bend over and pick up your toys. Pray for
someone who is having trouble moving.

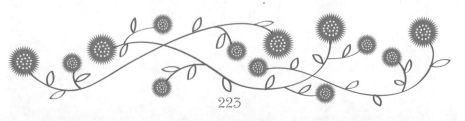

July 27

Animal Movements

Royal Words

God made all kinds of wild animals. He made all kinds of livestock. He made all kinds of creatures that move along the ground. And God saw that it was good.

GENESIS 1:25

Princess Thoughts

God made creatures that crawl, fly, hop, swim, dive, jump, run, and creep. He made cats and dogs that live with people. He made wild lions that live in jungles. God liked all the creatures he made.

A Prayer for the King

Father King, thanks for making so many types of animals. Some are little and furry. Some are big and scary. They are all your creatures.

Princess in Action

Move like different animals move. Flap your arms like a bird, crawl like a turtle, and swing like an elephant's trunk. Put some food out for animals that live near you. Put out some corn for deer, vegetable scraps for ducks, berries for birds, and nuts for squirrels.

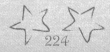

July 28

Tent Fun

Royal Words
Live in booths for seven days. All of the people of Israel must live in booths.
LEVITICUS 23:42

Princess Thoughts
Long ago God's people lived in a type of tent called a booth. After they moved and lived in houses, God wanted them to remember the days he cared for them when they lived in tents. He told them to spend a week camping and remembering him.

A Prayer for the King
Father King, help me to remember you and to remember that you take care of me.

Princess in Action
Camp out, or make a play tent with a blanket and table. Go inside the tent and think about how God takes care of you.

Jesus Goes with His Princess

Royal Words

[Jesus said,] "You can be sure that I am always with you, to the very end."

MATTHEW 28:20

Princess Thoughts

Jesus said he would always be with us. He is with you when you feel happy, sad, hurt, angry, or scared. He is also with you when you tell other people about him.

A Prayer for the King

Lord Jesus, thanks for always being with me. Help me to always listen to you.

Princess in Action

Get a magnet. See how it sticks to metal objects but not to other objects that are not metal. Jesus is like a magnet with believers. He sticks with anyone who believes in him.

Splashing Praises

Royal Words

Let heaven and earth praise him. Let the oceans and everything that moves in them praise him.

PSALM 69:34

Princess Thoughts

God made oceans that flow and waves that splash on the shore. He filled the seas with fish that swim, dolphins that jump high, and many other creatures that move. All the creatures God made can praise him as they show how creative he is.

A Prayer for the King

Father King, thank you for all you made, even the fish, whales, and crabs. Help me to see how creative you are when I look at what you made.

Princess in Action

Splash and swirl water in a bathtub, pool, lake, or ocean. Praise God for creating the ocean as you move in the water.

Graceful Movements

Royal Words
She is like a loving doe, a graceful deer.
PROVERBS 5:19

Princess Thoughts
Graceful means to move beautifully. A doe lifts her head and glides through the forest like a ballerina. A king compared the movements of the woman he loved to a beautiful, graceful deer.

A Prayer for the King
Father King, help me walk and move gracefully.

Princess in Action
Practice walking gracefully. Take smooth steps with your head up and back straight. You will be lovely to look at. God will smile as you move with grace.

August

A Special Ring

Royal Words

Pharaoh took his ring off his finger. It was the ring he used to stamp all of the official papers. He put it on Joseph's finger. He dressed him in robes that were made out of fine linen. He put a gold chain around his neck.

GENESIS 41:42

Princess Thoughts

Pharaoh wore a special ring. The ring could be dipped in melted wax and pressed on paper to show a special design. This seal showed that Pharaoh made the rule that was written on the paper. When Pharaoh gave this special ring to Joseph, it made Joseph very important. Pharaoh put Joseph in charge of all the food in Egypt.

A Prayer for the King

Father King, thanks for sparkling jewelry. I am thankful I am important to you.

Princess in Action

Thank God for making beautiful stones called jewels. Clean your favorite ring or piece of jewelry.

August 2

More Valuable Than Jewels

Royal Words
Who can find a noble wife? She is worth far more than rubies.
PROVERBS 31:10

Princess Thoughts
This part of the Bible talks about a loving and caring woman.
She's a good mother and wife. The Bible praises her.
The Bible says that this woman is more valuable than rubies,
which are fancy jewels.

A Prayer for the King
Father God, thanks for my mommy. Help her to be the best
mom she can be. Thanks for loving her.

Princess in Action
A ruby is red, the same color as our hearts and valentines.
Make a red heart for your mom. Tell her she is better than jewels.
Thank her for all she does for you.

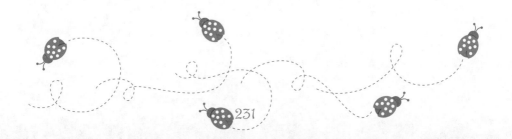

Ring of Love

Royal Words

But the father said to his servants, "Quick!
Bring the best robe and put it on him. Put a
ring on his finger and sandals on his feet."

LUKE 15:22

Princess Thoughts

A young man ran away from home and spent all his money.
He finally walked home, poor and hungry. The young man
started to tell his father he was sorry for what he did, but his
father stopped him. The father held a party to celebrate. He
had his servants put a ring on his son's finger. The ring
showed that the father loved his son and forgave him.

A Prayer for the King

Heavenly Father, thank you for loving me. Help me to stay
close to you and to my parents.

Princess in Action

God is like the father in the story. He loves us even when we
disobey. Wear a ring as a reminder of God's love.

God Sparkles

Royal Words

The One who sat there shone like jewels. Around the throne was a rainbow that looked like an emerald.

REVELATION 4:3

Princess Thoughts

God sits on a throne in heaven. The Bible tells us that God shines brightly, just like jewels sparkle in the light.

A Prayer for the King

Father King, you are better than sparkly jewels.

Princess in Action

Take a sparkle walk and see what shines or sparkles when the sun shines on it.

All Dolled Up

Royal Words

The people of Jerusalem will say, "We take great delight
in the LORD. We are joyful because we belong to our
God. He has dressed us with salvation as if it were our
clothes. He has put robes of godliness on us. We are
like a groom who is dressed up for his wedding. We are
like a bride who decorates herself with her jewels."

ISAIAH 61:10

Princess Thoughts

God's people will praise God and feel as happy as a beautiful
bride or princess all dressed up with sparkling jewels.
They will be happy because God has saved them.

A Prayer for the King

Father King, thanks for making me a beautiful princess.
I will praise you because I belong to you.

Princess in Action

Dress up and wear clothes and jewelry that sparkles.
Then sing songs to praise God.

The Best Treasure

Royal Words

[God's rules] are more priceless than gold. They have greater value than huge amounts of pure gold. They are sweeter than honey that is taken from the honeycomb.

PSALM 19:10

Princess Thoughts

God's words in the Bible show us how to have a good life. That is better than a treasure chest of jewels or the yummiest foods.

A Prayer for the King

Father King, thanks for your words. Help me to remember your rules and follow them.

Princess in Action

Let your mom or dad help you write today's verse on paper. Draw gold and jewels around the verse. Place the paper in your verse treasure box that you made on June 17 to remember to treasure God's words.

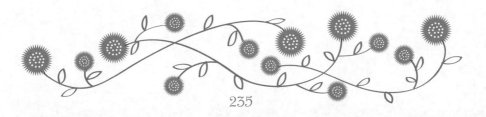

Jewels in a Crown

Royal Words

The LORD their God will save his people on that day.
They will be like sheep that belong to his flock. They
will gleam in his land like jewels in a crown.

ZECHARIAH 9:16

Princess Thoughts

God looks and sees his people sparkling like jewels.
We are precious to God. We belong to him, like
sheep belong to their shepherd.

A Prayer for the King

Lord God, I want to sparkle for you.

Princess in Action

Add a sparkling jewel to your princess treasure
chest that you made on July 1 as a reminder that
you are a precious princess to God.

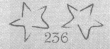

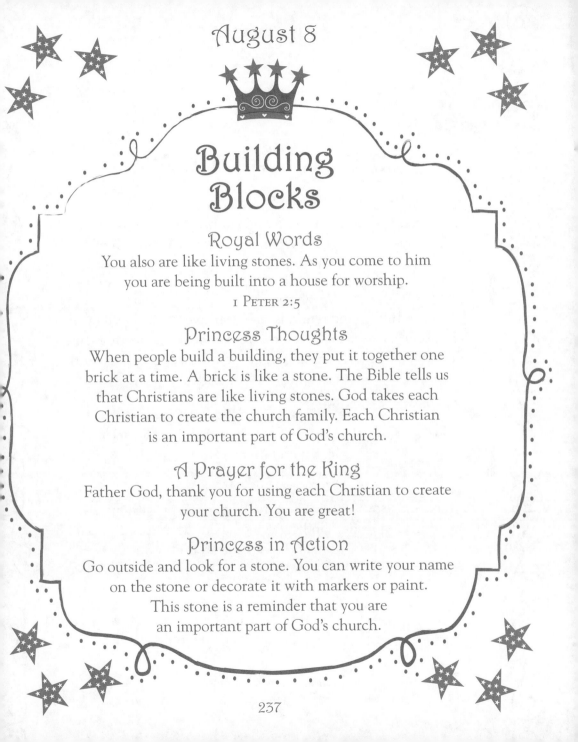

Building Blocks

Royal Words

You also are like living stones. As you come to him you are being built into a house for worship.

1 PETER 2:5

Princess Thoughts

When people build a building, they put it together one brick at a time. A brick is like a stone. The Bible tells us that Christians are like living stones. God takes each Christian to create the church family. Each Christian is an important part of God's church.

A Prayer for the King

Father God, thank you for using each Christian to create your church. You are great!

Princess in Action

Go outside and look for a stone. You can write your name on the stone or decorate it with markers or paint. This stone is a reminder that you are an important part of God's church.

Unseen Wonders

Royal Words

It is written, "No eye has seen, no ear has heard, no mind has known what God has prepared for those who love him."

1 CORINTHIANS 2:9

Princess Thoughts

In the Bible, God reminds us that heaven will be full of surprises that he is making for us to see, hear, and learn about. They will be more amazing than the wonders God made for us to enjoy here on earth.

A Prayer for the King

Father King, thanks for all you have prepared for me on earth and in heaven.

Princess in Action

Take an "I spy" walk. Take turns saying, "I spy with my eye something God made," and give clues about what it is. Spy out all sorts of wonders God made around you.

No More Tears

Royal Words

[God] will wipe away every tear from their eyes. There will be no more death or sadness. There will be no more crying or pain. Things are no longer the way they used to be.

REVELATION 21:4

Princess Thoughts

God tells us that there will be no tears and no pain in heaven. That's good news. Our sad times and tears on earth can help us appreciate happier times.

A Prayer for the King

Father King, thanks for wiping away my tears and letting me know a little more about heaven.

Princess in Action

Make a card for someone who is sad or sick. Let the person know that God cares.

Remember Past Sights

Royal Words

Don't be careless. Instead, be very careful. Don't forget the things your eyes have seen. As long as you live, don't let them slip from your mind. Teach them to your children and their children after them.

DEUTERONOMY 4:9

Princess Thoughts

The people of Israel saw God do many wonderful things. They knew how he answered their prayers. He wanted them to remember what he did and to tell their children about him. God wants us all to remember the prayers he answers and the wonderful things he does. He wants us to tell people how he answers prayers.

A Prayer for the King

Lord God, thanks for answering many prayers and making a beautiful world. Help me to tell others about prayers you answer.

Princess in Action

Ask your parents or grandparents to share what God has done for them. Draw pictures of their stories.

God's Choice

Royal Words

Do what is right and good in the LORD's eyes.
Then things will go well with you.
DEUTERONOMY 6:18

Princess Thoughts

God wants us to do what he says is right. Obeying God is
a good choice.

A Prayer for the King

Father King, help me to obey you and my parents.

Princess in Action

Play a game of choosing what is right in God's eyes. Let your
mom or dad give you two choices. See if you know which
choice is right in God's eyes.

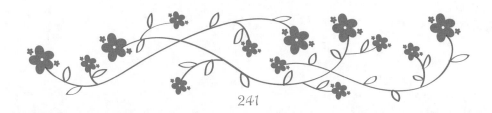

Straight Lines

Royal Words

Let your eyes look straight ahead. Keep
looking right in front of you.

PROVERBS 4:25

Princess Thoughts

Looking straight ahead means paying attention to where you
are going. It also means focusing on what you're doing instead
of getting distracted.

A Prayer for the King

Father King, thank you for my eyes. Help me to use them to
pay attention and to focus on doing my chores and learning
new things.

Princess in Action

Walk along a straight line. What happens if you look away
from the line or close your eyes as you try to walk on the line?
How does it help to look at the line as you walk? Look at
what you are doing as you do chores or learn a new skill.

Pay Attention

Royal Words

[Boaz said to Ruth,] "Keep your eye on the field where
the men are cutting grain. Walk behind the women
who are gathering it. Pick up the grain that is left."
RUTH 2:9

Princess Thoughts

A rule during Bible times allowed poor people to gather food left
by the harvesters. A poor woman named Ruth went to a field
where men cut grain. She followed behind to pick up the leftovers.
Boaz, the owner of the field, told Ruth he would take care of her.

A Prayer for the King

Father King, you care about poor and hungry people. Help me to
pay attention to people who are poor and hungry.

Princess in Action

Help your mommy or daddy pick out some canned and packaged
foods in your cupboards to make a care package. Give the food
to someone who needs it. Or you could give the care package
to a food pantry.

August 15

Be Careful, Little Eyes

Royal Words

Turn my eyes away from things that are worthless.

PSALM 119:37

Princess Thoughts

The words above are from the longest psalm in the Bible. A psalm is a type of song. This psalm praises God's Word. The words in this verse remind us to stop looking at what is not good for us. God can help us to think carefully about what we look at.

A Prayer for the King

Lord God, thanks for my eyesight. Help me to make wise choices about what to look at with my eyes.

Princess in Action

Talk with your mom and dad about what you watch on television. Don't watch shows that are not good to see, such as ones that have people hurting or teasing other people. Choose shows that have people talking nicely to each other.

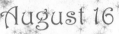

August 16

Truth

Royal Words

Open my eyes so that I can see the wonderful truths in your law.
PSALM 119:18

Princess Thoughts

God wants every princess to open her eyes to learn wisdom from
the Bible. This means that God wants you to pay attention to
what the Bible says.

A Prayer for the King

Father King, thanks for sharing great wisdom in the Bible.
Help me to pay attention to what you teach me.

Princess in Action

Play a truth game. Let your mom or dad state two facts, one
that is true and one that is made up. See if you can guess
which one is true. God's Word is always true.

God Watches over You

Royal Words

The eyes of the Lord are everywhere. They watch those who are evil and those who are good.

PROVERBS 15:3

Princess Thoughts

God sees everyone. He watches us and knows what we do and how we behave. God loves to see his princess obey her parents. He loves to see his princess be polite and kind.

A Prayer for the King

Father King, thank you for watching over everyone. Help me to choose to do what's good.

Princess in Action

Add sparkling little jewels to sunglasses, or put stickers on the rims. Put on the sunglasses, and remember God is watching over you.

Eye Circles

Royal Words

My face is red from crying. I have deep circles under my eyes.

Job 16:16

Princess Thoughts

When you cry a long time, you may look in a mirror and
see that your eyes look red and puffy. There may be dark
circles under your eyes. A man in the Bible named Job
cried a lot because he was sad and hurting.

A Prayer for the King

Dear God, thanks for my eyes. When I am sad and
crying, help me to feel better.

Princess in Action

Talk about what makes you cry. After you cry, it helps to
cover your eyes with a cool, wet washcloth.

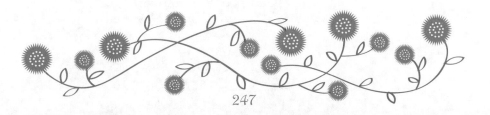

Prayer Book

Royal Words
After Job had prayed for his friends, the LORD made him
successful again. He gave him twice as much as he had before.
JOB 42:10

Princess Thoughts
Job had a terrible day. He lost his children, his animals, and his
money. Job's friends came to comfort Job. After many days,
God spoke to Job and helped him feel better. Then Job prayed
for his friends. God gave Job more children, lots more animals,
and more money.

A Prayer for the King
Father King, help me to talk to you when things go wrong.
Thanks for friends who care about how I feel.
Help me to pray for my friends.

Princess in Action
Make a prayer book. Draw or put in pictures of family, friends,
food, your home, your church, clothes, toys, and other things.
Use the book to thank God for the things you have
and to pray for people you love.

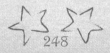

August 20

Real Friends

Royal Words

A friend loves at all times. He is there
to help when trouble comes.

PROVERBS 17:17

Princess Thoughts

God's Word helps us to know how to be a real friend.
We are to love our friends all the time and forgive them
even if they hurt our feelings. And we should be there to
help when our friends have problems.

A Prayer for the King

Lord Jesus, thanks for giving me friends. Help me to be
a good friend.

Princess in Action

Practice being a good friend today. If your friend is
sad, give her a hug. Let your friend have the first
turn in games.

Precious Friends

Royal Words

My brothers and sisters, that is how you should stand firm in the Lord's strength. I love you and long for you. Dear friends, you are my joy and my crown.

PHILIPPIANS 4:1

Princess Thoughts

The apostle Paul wrote to his friends. His letter is part of the Bible. He loved his friends and missed them when he wasn't with them. Paul's friends made his heart happy. They were like very valuable jewels in a king's crown.

A Prayer for the King

Father King, thank you for my friends. Help me to tell them how special they are.

Princess in Action

Let your friends know they are special. Make a crown to give to each of your friends. Put some of their names on your own princess crown to remember that your friends are as valuable as jewels.

Love and Friends

Royal Words

Dear friends, let us love one another, because love comes from God. Everyone who loves has been born again because of what God has done. That person knows God.

1 JOHN 4:7

Princess Thoughts

God wants us to love people because he made them and because he loves them. God created love. He wants us to share that love with others.

A Prayer for the King

Father King, thanks for loving all people. Help me to love the people you made.

Princess in Action

A princess loves the people that God the King loves. Buy stickers that tell about God's love, and stick them on envelopes your mom or dad plan to mail. Mail cards to friends, and send them stickers.

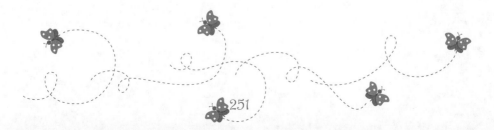

A Special Friend

Royal Words

The Father will send the Friend in my name to help you.
The Friend is the Holy Spirit. He will teach you all things.
He will remind you of everything I have said to you.

JOHN 14:26

Princess Thoughts

Jesus promised to send every believer a special friend, the Holy
Spirit. We don't see the Holy Spirit, but he is with us and helps us.
The Holy Spirit reminds us of what Jesus taught.

A Prayer for the King

Lord Jesus, thanks for sending your special friend to remind me
of what you have said and what you will do.

Princess in Action

A dove is the symbol for the Holy Spirit. When John the
Baptist baptized Jesus, the Holy Spirit came down from
heaven and looked like a dove. (You can read about that in
the Bible, in Mark 1.) Find a white feather, or cut a white
paper feather. Put it in your princess treasure chest that you
made on July 1 as a reminder of the Holy Spirit.

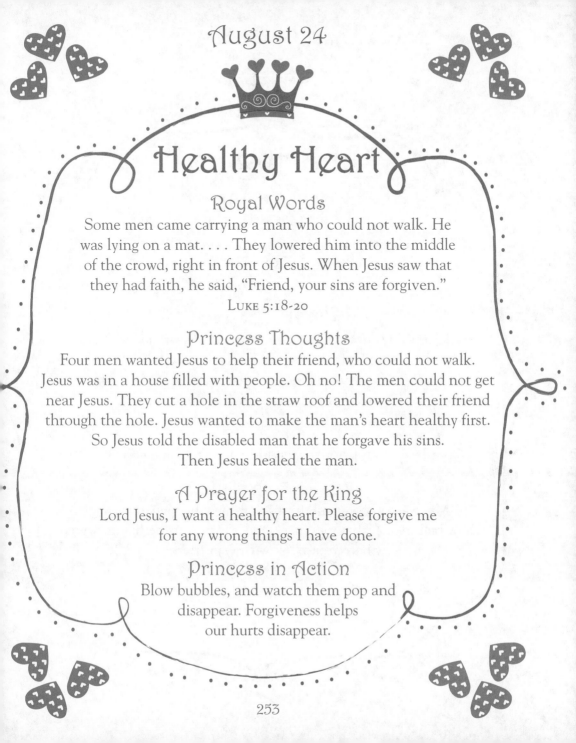

Healthy Heart

Royal Words

Some men came carrying a man who could not walk. He was lying on a mat. . . . They lowered him into the middle of the crowd, right in front of Jesus. When Jesus saw that they had faith, he said, "Friend, your sins are forgiven."

LUKE 5:18-20

Princess Thoughts

Four men wanted Jesus to help their friend, who could not walk. Jesus was in a house filled with people. Oh no! The men could not get near Jesus. They cut a hole in the straw roof and lowered their friend through the hole. Jesus wanted to make the man's heart healthy first. So Jesus told the disabled man that he forgave his sins. Then Jesus healed the man.

A Prayer for the King

Lord Jesus, I want a healthy heart. Please forgive me for any wrong things I have done.

Princess in Action

Blow bubbles, and watch them pop and disappear. Forgiveness helps our hurts disappear.

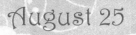

Sharing Joy

Royal Words

When she finds [the lost coin], she will call her friends and neighbors together. She will say, "Be joyful with me. I have found my lost coin."

LUKE 15:9

Princess Thoughts

Jesus told the story about a woman who searched for her lost money. She looked everywhere and swept her house. After finding the coin, the woman was very happy. She wanted her friends to celebrate with her.

A Prayer for the King

Lord Jesus, thank you for reminding me to share good news.

Princess in Action

Make a book of good things that have happened to you. Draw pictures of what God has done and prayers he has answered. Share your book with your friends.

Being Friendly

Royal Words

Greet each other with a friendly kiss. May God give
peace to all of you who believe in Christ.

1 PETER 5:14

Princess Thoughts

Blowing a kiss to someone is a friendly kiss. So is a kiss
on the cheek. God wants us to be friendly and to greet
other people kindly. It's also good to say hi to people
at church.

A Prayer for the King

Father King, help me be kind to everyone.

Princess in Action

Practice being friendly to people today. Blow kisses
to your friends and family.

Don't Worry— Pray!

Royal Words

About midnight Paul and Silas were praying. They were also singing hymns to God. The other prisoners were listening to them.

ACTS 16:25

Princess Thoughts

Men threw Paul and his friend in jail because they talked about Jesus. Paul and his friend didn't worry. They prayed and sang. Paul knew that Christians can pray anywhere instead of worrying. God heard Paul and his friend and saved them.

A Prayer for the King

Father King, thank you for being with us even when bad things happen. Help me to trust you instead of worrying.

Princess in Action

Paul and Silas had to wear chains around their wrists when they were in prison. Wear a bracelet around your wrist as a reminder to pray instead of worrying.

The Shepherd's Voice

Royal Words

[Jesus said,] "When [the shepherd] has brought all of his own sheep out, he goes on ahead of them. His sheep follow him because they know his voice. . . . I am the good shepherd."

JOHN 10:4, 11

Princess Thoughts

Jesus told people that sheep learn to recognize their shepherd's voice and respond to it. Jesus also said that he is our shepherd. We will learn to recognize and follow his voice.

A Prayer for the King

Lord Jesus, thank you for calling me one of your sheep. Help me to learn to know your voice and follow it.

Princess in Action

Jesus is your shepherd. As you pray and read God's Word, you will learn to recognize his voice. Play Follow the Leader today, and talk about ways to follow Jesus. Bleat like a lamb as you play.

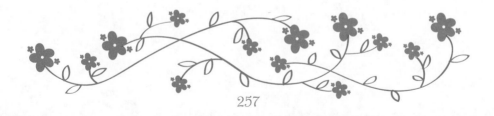

Run from Strangers

Royal Words

[Sheep] will never follow a stranger. In fact, they will run away from him. They don't recognize a stranger's voice.

JOHN 10:5

Princess Thoughts

Jesus, our Good Shepherd, told people that sheep run from strangers. Running away from an unfamiliar voice keeps the sheep safe. Jesus wants his followers to turn away when they hear a voice they don't know.

A Prayer for the King

Lord Jesus, thank you for wanting to keep me safe.

Princess in Action

Talk to your parents about people you do not know. Talk about which strangers can help you and which strangers you should stay away from.

August 30

Staying Safe

Royal Words

[God,] save me. Set me free from strangers who
attack me. They tell all kinds of lies with their
mouths. Even when they make a promise by
raising their right hands, they don't mean it.

PSALM 144:11

Princess Thoughts

God's Word talks about some strangers who are not nice and
actually want to hurt people. They lie and make false promises.
The words in today's verse are also a prayer to ask God for
protection from bad people.

A Prayer for the King

Father God, protect me from bad people.

Princess in Action

Yesterday, you talked about rules you should follow when you meet
a stranger. These rules help keep you safe. Wear a red jewel to
remind you of your parents' rules.

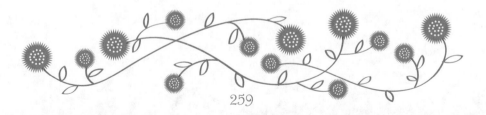

Protection

Royal Words

[God,] take good care of me, just as you would take care of
your own eyes. Hide me in the shadow of your wings.

PSALM 17:8

Princess Thoughts

The shadow of God's wings is a picture. It helps us understand
how God protects us. A mother bird covers her baby with her
wings to protect it, especially from rain and wind. God cares
for you like a mother bird cares for her baby.

A Prayer for the King

Father King, thank you for protecting me, your princess.

Princess in Action

Take care of your eyes. Go wash them with a warm, wet
washcloth. When you go outside today, wear a hat with a
visor or sunglasses in the bright sun. Chat about how your
parents protect you and how God protects you.

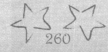

September

Princess Diary

Royal Words

The other events of Solomon's rule are written down.
Everything he did and the wisdom he showed are written
down. They are written in the official records of Solomon.

1 Kings 11:41

Princess Thoughts

King Solomon wrote about what he did. God used Solomon to
write wise words in Proverbs and other parts of the Bible.
Solomon's words still lead God's people with wisdom.

A Prayer for the King

Father King, thanks for giving me the ability to learn how to read
and write. Thank you for the great wisdom in the Bible.

Princess in Action

A diary is a book to keep a record of what you do and think
and learn about God. It's a place to write or draw your
prayers, too. Ask your mom or dad if you can get or make a
diary. Decorate the cover with glitter, beads, or sequins.
Draw pictures of your day in the diary.

September 2

Joyful Thoughts

Royal Words
We are writing this to make our joy complete.
1 John 1:4

Princess Thoughts
God gave us the Bible to help us learn how to make wise choices. God also gave us the Bible to bring us joy. The Bible shares what happened to Jesus, what God has done, and how much God loves us. That makes us happy. The Bible is sometimes called the Word of Life because the words help people live better.

A Prayer for the King
Father God, thanks for sharing about Jesus in the Bible so all people can know Jesus and know joy.

Princess in Action
Write in your diary that you started on September 1 things that make you smile or laugh. Share those happy thoughts with other people so they can be joyful too.

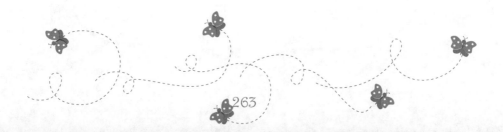

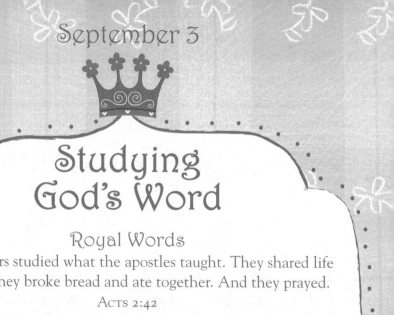

Studying God's Word

Royal Words

The believers studied what the apostles taught. They shared life together. They broke bread and ate together. And they prayed.

Acts 2:42

Princess Thoughts

Christians study the Bible because it tells us what God did and what God wants us to know. The first Christians ate meals together and prayed together. Christians love one another and share life together.

A Prayer for the King

Father King, thanks for people who believe in you and come together at church to share your love and to study the Bible.

Princess in Action

Make friends with people at church and Sunday school. Study the Bible with them. Add the names or pictures of church friends to your diary that you started on September 1.

September 4

Wisdom

Royal Words

Your heart will become wise. Your mind
will delight in knowledge.

PROVERBS 2:10

Princess Thoughts

When you learn what's in the Bible, your mind is filled with good
things to think about. The Bible helps you to be wise. Wisdom
helps you make good choices.

A Prayer for the King

Father King, help me to learn and remember your
words from the Bible.

Princess in Action

Talk about a favorite Bible story and how it has helped
you to be wise and make good choices. Write about it
or draw it in your diary from September 1.

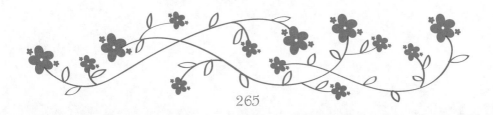

What God Studies

Royal Words

The LORD says, "I look deep down inside human hearts. I see what is in people's minds."
JEREMIAH 17:10

Princess Thoughts

God looks into people's hearts and minds. He knows what you think and how you feel. God cares about your thoughts because you are his princess.

A Prayer for the King

Father God, help me to think about good things.

Princess in Action

With help, write in your diary that you started on September 1 about how you feel. Write or draw what you think about today's verse.

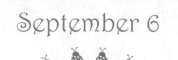

September 6

Keeping Promises

Royal Words

God isn't a mere man. He can't lie. He isn't a human
being. He doesn't change his mind. He speaks, and then
he acts. He makes a promise, and then he keeps it.

Numbers 23:19

Princess Thoughts

Sometimes people lie or break promises, but God always
keeps his word. He always speaks the truth. We can believe
all that is in the Bible because it comes from God.

A Prayer for the King

Father King, thanks for always keeping your promises.
Help me to be faithful to keep my promises.

Princess in Action

Talk about promises and what you have promised your mom or
dad. In your diary that you started on September 1, draw pictures
of rules you promise to follow. Work on one
promise, such as a promise to put your
toys away before bedtime.

September 7

Favorite Things

Royal Words

Don't live any longer the way this world lives.
Let your way of thinking be completely changed.
Then you will be able to test what God wants for
you. And you will agree that what he wants is
right. His plan is good and pleasing and perfect.

ROMANS 12:2

Princess Thoughts

If you think about a toy you want all the time, you
probably will not enjoy the toys you already have. What
you think about makes a difference in how you act.
Enjoy what you do have.

A Prayer for the King

Father King, I am happy that you love me. Thank you
for blessing me with a home, family, and toys. Help me
to enjoy what I have.

Princess in Action

In your princess diary from September 1 draw pictures of
your favorite toys, books, and friends. Thank God for
each one.

September 8

The Royal Diary

Royal Words

That night [King Xerxes] couldn't sleep. So he
ordered the official records of his rule to be brought
in. He ordered someone to read them to him.

ESTHER 6:1

Princess Thoughts

King Xerxes listened as someone read his diary. The words
reminded him of when a man named Mordecai saved his life. The
king ordered that people honor Mordecai with a parade.

A Prayer for the King

Father God, remind me of people who have done good things for
me so I can honor them.

Princess in Action

Look through your princess diary that you started on September 1,
and remember what good things God and other people have done
for you. Send a special thank-you note to the people. Write a
thank-you note to God in your diary.

269

Beautiful Words

Royal Words

My heart is full of beautiful words as I say my poem for the king. My tongue is like the pen of a skillful writer.

PSALM 45:1

Princess Thoughts

The Bible reminds us that the words we say are like the words of a writer. When we think about good things, we speak beautiful words.

A Prayer for the King

Father King, thank you for the gift of words. Help me to use my tongue to say beautiful words.

Princess in Action

Create a poem, rhyme, or song. Let someone help you write the words. Talk about the letter sounds at the beginning of some of the words. Share the poem or song with friends.

September 10

The Holy Spirit Prays

Royal Words

The Holy Spirit helps us when we are weak. We don't know what we should pray for. But the Spirit himself prays for us. He prays with groans too deep for words.

ROMANS 8:26

Princess Thoughts

God sent us a special helper, his Holy Spirit. The Holy Spirit prays for us when we don't know what to say to God. If you are too upset or too sad to pray, ask the Holy Spirit for help. The Holy Spirit will pray for you.

A Prayer for the King

Father King, thanks for sending your Holy Spirit to pray for me.

Princess in Action

Ask your mom or dad for help. He or she can help you reach something that's too high or drive you to see a friend. Talk about how it's great to have help and how it's good that Jesus sent his special helper, the Holy Spirit.

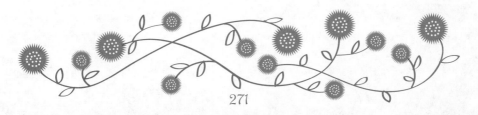

Celebrate Hope

Royal Words

Give praise to the God and Father of our Lord Jesus Christ. In his great mercy he has given us a new birth and a hope that is alive. It is alive because Jesus Christ rose from the dead.

1 PETER 1:3

Princess Thoughts

Hope means to expect something good. We have hope because we know Jesus rose from the dead so we could live in heaven forever. That's a reason to praise God and to be happy.

A Prayer for the King

Lord Jesus, thanks for giving me hope for a great future in heaven.

Princess in Action

Celebrate hope with a praise parade. March around cheering that Jesus rose and that you will go to heaven. Ask your mom or dad to take a photo of your praise parade, and put it in your diary that you started on September 1.

September 12

Trouble and Bad Days

Royal Words

Anyone who does what is right may have many troubles. But the LORD saves him from all of them.

PSALM 34:19

Princess Thoughts

God says we can do what's right and still have problems or bad days. But God promises to help us with the problems. He's with us on our bad days.

A Prayer for the King

Father King, please help me when I have a bad day.

Princess in Action

Work on a puzzle book or maze and see how you can solve a problem. God is even better at solving problems. He wants to help you.

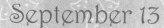

Cheerleaders

Royal Words
Cheer each other up with the hope you have. Build each other up. In fact, that's what you are doing.
1 Thessalonians 5:11

Princess Thoughts
God wants us to be cheerleaders and to encourage people. We share hope when we cheer people on. We can build others up by sharing the hope Jesus gives us.

A Prayer for the King
Lord Jesus, help me to be a good cheerleader.

Princess in Action
Cheer for your friends and family. Say "Jesus loves you!" when someone is sad.

September 14

Graceful Words

Royal Words

Let the words you speak always be full of grace. Season them
with salt. Then you will know how to answer everyone.

COLOSSIANS 4:6

Princess Thoughts

Salt brings out the flavor in foods. God wants our words to bring
out the best in people. He wants our words to be full of grace.
That means we should speak with love and care, and we should
talk about how God is part of our lives.

A Prayer for the King

Father King, help me to speak with grace and show your love
through my words.

Princess in Action

Eat popcorn without salt. Then eat some with salt. How
does the popcorn taste without salt? How does it taste
with salt? Sprinkle joy and kindness in people's lives to
bring out the best in them.

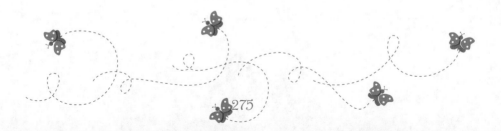

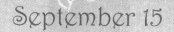

September 15

Finding Scriptures

Royal Words

The LORD said to Moses, "Write down the words I have spoken. I have made a covenant with you and with Israel in keeping with those words."

EXODUS 34:27

Princess Thoughts

God told Moses to write down what he told him. The words included a special agreement between God and his people. This agreement is called a covenant. Written words help people remember them.

A Prayer for the King

Father King, I'm thankful we can read in the Bible the words you gave to Moses.

Princess in Action

Have your mom or dad write some of your favorite Bible verses in your diary that you started on September 1. You can go back and read the verses to remember God's promises to you.

276

September 16

Bad Dreams

Royal Words

In the second year of Nebuchadnezzar's rule, he had a
dream. His mind was troubled. He couldn't sleep.

DANIEL 2:1

Princess Thoughts

A bad dream makes it hard to sleep. King Nebuchadnezzar
dreamed about a statue. The dream worried the king. He would
not tell others what his dream was about. But God told Daniel
what the dream was about. This special dream was a message from
God about the future. Daniel explained the meaning of the dream
to King Nebuchadnezzar.

A Prayer for the King

Father King, please help me not to be upset by bad dreams.
Thank you for always being with me.

Princess in Action

If a dream upsets you, describe it to your mom or dad.
Draw a picture of the dream. Ask God to help you
not to worry about the dream.

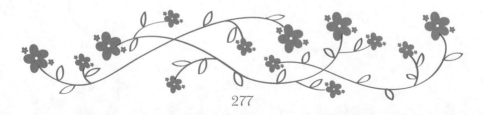

No Arguing

Royal Words
Do everything without finding fault or arguing.
PHILIPPIANS 2:14

Princess Thoughts
God wants us to avoid arguing with people. He doesn't want us to point out mistakes people make or to make fun of other people. God wants us to always look for something good to say.

A Prayer for the King
Dear Lord, help me to find good things about people. Please help me not to argue with others.

Princess in Action
Practice obedience today. When your mom or dad asks you to do something, obey without arguing.

September 18

Happy Thoughts

Royal Words

Always think about what is true. Think about what is
noble, right and pure. Think about what is lovely and
worthy of respect. If anything is excellent or worthy
of praise, think about those kinds of things.

PHILIPPIANS 4:8

Princess Thoughts

God wants us to think about good things. That means to think
about Bible verses, nice words to say, and good things to do.

A Prayer for the King

Father King, you are always kind to me, your princess. Help me
to think about you and to think about good things.

Princess in Action

With help from your mom or dad, make a list of good things
to think about. Cut out pictures of good things to think about,
and put them in your diary that you started on September 1.
Then, if you start to whine, argue, or complain, stop talking.
Go look at the pictures of good things in your diary.

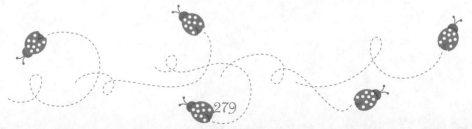

September 19

Heavenly Thoughts

Royal Words
The Son of Man will come in all his glory. All
the angels will come with him. Then he will
sit on his throne in the glory of heaven.
MATTHEW 25:31

Princess Thoughts
Jesus talked about heaven as a wonderful place. Heaven
is filled with angels and people who love Jesus. If you
love Jesus, you will also go to heaven.

A Prayer for the King
Father King, thanks for making heaven and filling it
with people who love you.

Princess in Action
Name people you know who love Jesus. Thank God for each one.
They will go to heaven!

September 20

Heavenly Wisdom

Royal Words

The wisdom that comes from heaven is pure. That's the most important thing about it. And that's not all. It also loves peace. It thinks about others. It obeys. It is full of mercy and good fruit. It is fair. It doesn't pretend to be what it is not.

JAMES 3:17

Princess Thoughts

It's good to be smart, but being wise is better. God's wisdom brings peace. It helps us to remember to obey God's rules. We get his wisdom when we read the Bible and do what it says. God's wisdom helps us to be fair and make peace.

A Prayer for the King

Lord God, thanks for wisdom that helps me to obey and have peace.

Princess in Action

Wisdom from God helps us to think about other people. Talk with your mom or dad about ways you can help today.

How to Get Wisdom

Royal Words

If any of you need wisdom, ask God for it. He will give it to you. God gives freely to everyone. He doesn't find fault.

JAMES 1:5

Princess Thoughts

People don't know everything, but God does. He loves you, his princess, and he wants to help you. When you don't know how to solve a problem, ask God for wisdom.

A Prayer for the King

Father King, thanks for sharing your wisdom when I pray and ask you for help.

Princess in Action

Put a puzzle together with your mom or dad. Did you need to ask your mom or dad for help to put it together? When you need help from God, ask him for it.

September 22

Understanding Hearts

Royal Words
[God said to Solomon,] "I will give you a
wise and understanding heart."
1 Kings 3:12

Princess Thoughts
Solomon became king of Israel. He prayed and gave God many
offerings. God asked Solomon what he wanted most. Solomon said
he wanted a wise and understanding heart to lead God's people
well. So God made Solomon the wisest man who ever lived.

A Prayer for the King
Father King, fill my heart and mind with wisdom.
Help me to use wisdom to help people.

Princess in Action
Talk with your mom or dad about ways to use wisdom. Share
what you know with a younger child. Maybe you could help
that child play a game. Understand that the child still needs
to learn, so be gentle and patient.

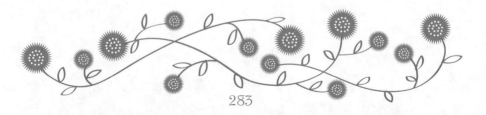

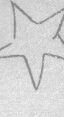

September 23

Peaceful Minds

Royal Words
The mind controlled by the Spirit brings life and peace.
ROMANS 8:6

Princess Thoughts
God lets us know how we can have peace.
It begins in our minds. If we let the Holy Spirit guide us, we will
have peace. The Holy Spirit can help us make decisions.
We will not spend time worrying or arguing.

A Prayer for the King
Father King, may your Holy Spirit guide my thoughts.

Princess in Action
Take a peace walk. Look for signs of peace as you walk
(smiling people, playful creatures, calm water, clear sky).

Right Choices Bring Peace

Royal Words

Doing what is right will bring peace and rest. When my people do that, they will stay calm and trust in the Lord forever.

Isaiah 32:17

Princess Thoughts

Doing what is right is good. Your home will be quiet and peaceful if you don't argue or whine. It's good to learn how to be calm even when you don't get your way. Instead of getting angry and yelling, learn ways to keep yourself calm.

A Prayer for the King

Father God, help me choose to do what is right to help bring peace.

Princess in Action

Practice calming down. Take deep breaths, while tapping each of your ten fingers.

September 25

Living in Peace

Royal Words

If possible, live in peace with everyone.
Do that as much as you can.

ROMANS 12:18

Princess Thoughts

God wants us to work at living in peace with other
people. If someone is grouchy or says something to hurt
you, smile and forgive the person. If someone wants a
toy you are using, share it. Saying kind words that help
people feel better brings peace too.

A Prayer for the King

Father King, help me to live in peace with people.

Princess in Action

Look and see what you can do to make other people
happy. Think of a compliment to give each person, such
as telling a friend she has a nice smile or pretty eyes.

Following Rules

Royal Words
If you train your children, they will give you
peace. They will bring delight to you.
PROVERBS 29:17

Princess Thoughts
The Bible includes special words for moms and dads on
how to be good parents. Training a child means to teach
him or her. Parents teach children to follow rules, play
games, clean up toys, cook, and be polite. Daughters and
sons who listen and learn make their parents happy.

A Prayer for the King
Father King, help me to listen to my parents and
learn from them.

Princess in Action
Talk to your mom and dad about the rule you have the
most trouble following. Practice following that rule.

Answered Prayers

Royal Words

I have told you these things, so that you can have peace because of me. In this world you will have trouble. But cheer up! I have won the battle over the world.

JOHN 16:33

Princess Thoughts

God does not promise that we will be happy all the time. He knows we will be sad sometimes. He wants us to remember he is always with us, even when we're sad.

A Prayer for the King

Dear Jesus, thanks for helping me when I am sad.

Princess in Action

Draw a picture of how God has helped you when you were sad. When you have new problems, remember that God is always with you. Draw a cross next to your picture to remind you that God understands your sadness and that he is with you.

September 28

Work for Peace

Royal Words

Let us do all we can to live in peace. And let
us work hard to build each other up.

ROMANS 14:19

Princess Thoughts

We have peace when people get along. To build people up
means to encourage them, to praise them for what they do
well. We can get along with people when we encourage them.

A Prayer for the King

Father King, help me to build up other people.

Princess in Action

Become a good-deed spy. Look out for when someone
does something well, then praise the action. Tell your
mom she cooked a good meal. Thank your dad for
keeping you safe in the car on a trip.

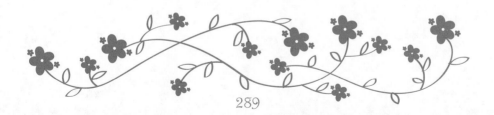

Peace and Order

Royal Words
God is not a God of disorder. He is a God of peace.
1 CORINTHIANS 14:33

Princess Thoughts
Before God created the world, there was only darkness and chaos.
But God made beauty and order when he created the world. When
your room is a mess, it's hard to find things in the middle of the
chaos. When toys, books, and other items are in order, it's easier
to find an item. That makes life more peaceful.

A Prayer for the King
Creator God, thanks for being organized.
Help me to keep my things in order.

Princess in Action
Put your books in order so you can find favorite ones more easily.
Group the same types, such as putting all the
animal books together.

What Causes Fights?

Royal Words

Why do you fight and argue among yourselves? Isn't it because of your sinful longings? They fight inside you.

JAMES 4:1

Princess Thoughts

God's Word talks about why people fight and argue. We fight because we want our own way. We want the newest toy, the biggest slice of cake, or the first turn in a game. It's not good to want our own way, especially if it hurts other people.

A Prayer for the King

Father King, help me to think of other people and your way instead of wanting my own way.

Princess in Action

Divide a snack or cake, and let other people choose their pieces first. Thank God for your treat. Eat slowly and enjoy each bite.

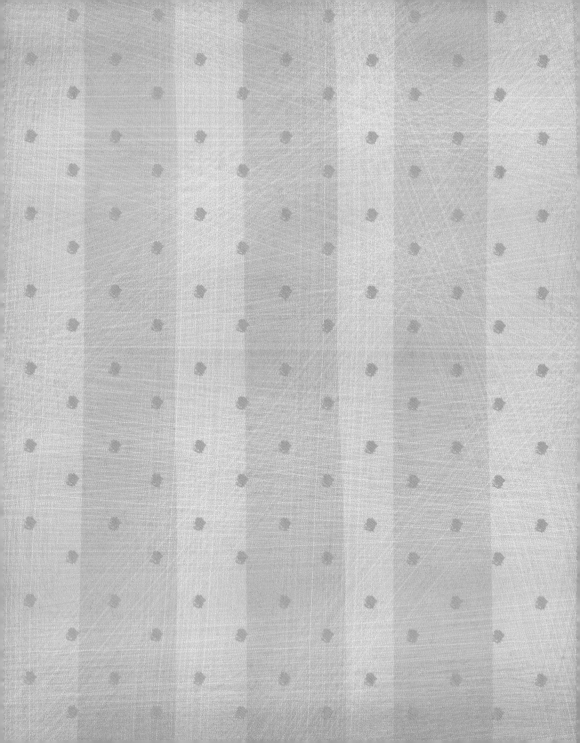

October

Princess Feet

Royal Words

The king says to the Shulammite woman, "You are like a prince's daughter. Your feet in sandals are so beautiful. Your graceful legs are like jewels. The hands of a skilled worker must have shaped them."

SONG OF SONGS 7:1

Princess Thoughts

The king noticed his bride's beautiful feet and legs. God made the bride's feet and legs. He made your feet and legs too. You can use your feet and legs to walk, dance, run, hop, and stand. Your feet are the feet of a princess.

A Prayer for the King

Father King, thanks for making feet and legs that move. Show me how to use them to help other people.

Princess in Action

God made your beautiful feet and legs. Practice the things you can do with your feet and legs. (Hint: You can hop, walk, dance, and run.)

294

Beautiful Feet

Royal Words
It is written, "How beautiful are the feet
of those who bring good news!"
ROMANS 10:15

Princess Thoughts
According to the Bible, the most beautiful feet belong to people
who bring the good news that God loves us. God wants his people
to share the good news about Jesus.

A Prayer for the King
Father God, thanks for my beautiful feet. Help me to share the
good news of your love with everyone I see today.

Princess in Action
Make cards with hearts on them. Have a grown-up write
"God loves you" on the cards. Use your feet to go and give
the good-news cards to people.

Shoe Check

Royal Words

Put on all of God's armor. . . . Wear on your feet what
will prepare you to tell the good news of peace.

EPHESIANS 6:13, 15

Princess Thoughts

The Bible tells us about a special set of armor we can wear
when sharing the Good News. This armor helps us to be
prepared and includes things like truth and salvation. When
we are going to share the Good News, we can picture
ourselves putting this armor on. We can picture wearing safe,
comfortable shoes so we are ready to walk and share the
news of peace.

A Prayer for the King

Father King, please keep my feet safe as I travel.

Princess in Action

Practice putting on your shoes so you can protect your
feet when you go outside.

October 4

Washing Feet

Royal Words

[A widow] must be well known for the good things she does.
That includes bringing up children. It includes inviting
guests into her home. It includes washing the feet of God's
people. It includes helping those who are in trouble.

1 Timothy 5:10

Princess Thoughts

Today's Bible verse talks about the good things a widow should do.
(A widow is a woman whose husband has died.) In Bible times,
people wore sandals and walked on dirt streets, so their feet got
dirty. A widow was expected to wash her guests' feet. God wants
all princesses to welcome guests and do good deeds.

A Prayer for the King

Father King, thanks for widows and older women who follow you.
Help me to serve you all my life.

Princess in Action

Help your parents get your home ready for guests. Be sure to have
soap and a clean towel in the bathroom. If your guests use the
bathroom, they have what they need to wash their hands.

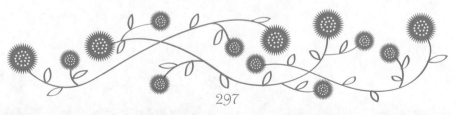

Deer Feet

Royal Words
[God] makes my feet like the feet of a deer. He
helps me stand on the highest places.
2 SAMUEL 22:34

Princess Thoughts
Deer have graceful and fast feet. They move quietly, and
they easily glide through the air. Deer are very good at
balancing because of their feet. Deer can climb
mountains without slipping. They can stand at edges
of cliffs and not be afraid of falling.

A Prayer for the King
Father King, help me to run fast and gracefully.
Help me to balance and not fall.

Princess in Action
Practice balancing. Stand on one foot. Raise and lower
each leg sideways. Jump up and down.

October 6

Standing Up

Royal Words
Jesus took him by the hand. He lifted the boy
to his feet, and the boy stood up.

MARK 9:27

Princess Thoughts
A man brought his son to Jesus for healing. An evil
spirit made the boy foam at the mouth and become stiff
and unable to move. Jesus healed the boy and lifted him
to his feet. Hooray for Jesus!

A Prayer for the King
Lord Jesus, you are amazing. Heal the people
I love when they are sick.

Princess in Action
With your mom or dad's help, trace your foot on paper.
Cut the foot out. On the paper foot, draw or write a
thank-you note to Jesus. Thank Jesus for helping the boy
in the Bible story to stand. Thank Jesus for healing other
people too.

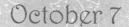

Sweet Feet

Royal Words

I, your Lord and Teacher, have washed your feet.
So you also should wash one another's feet.

JOHN 13:14

Princess Thoughts

Jesus washed the feet of his friends. They must have had
clean and sweet-smelling feet then! He also told his
friends that they should wash each other's feet. Jesus
wants people to care for one another.

A Prayer for the King

Lord Jesus, help me to care for other people.

Princess in Action

Do something special for your mom's feet. Help fill the
bathtub for a bubble bath. Put out a towel and nice
lotion for your mom to use after her bath.

Perfumed Feet

Royal Words

She stood behind Jesus and cried at his feet. She began to wet his feet with her tears. Then she wiped them with her hair. She kissed them and poured perfume on them.

LUKE 7:38

Princess Thoughts

This woman felt very thankful that Jesus forgave her sins and that he cared for her. She showed her love by washing his feet and pouring expensive perfume on them. She dried his feet with her long hair.

A Prayer for the King

Lord Jesus, thank you for loving me. Help me to show you that I love you.

Princess in Action

Show Jesus you love him. Cut a heart from craft foam or paper. Cut a hole in the heart to fit over a doorknob. Every time you open the door, say, "I love you, Jesus."

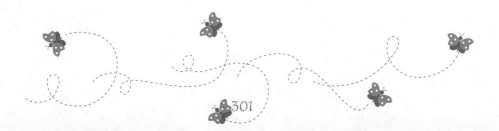

October 9

Directions

Royal Words
I will walk among you. I will be your God.
And you will be my people.
LEVITICUS 26:12

Princess Thoughts
In the Bible, God says he will walk among us. That means he will be with us all the time. Although we can't see God, we can know that he is with us.

A Prayer for the King
Father God, thank you for walking with me.

Princess in Action
Take a walk and let your mom or dad tell you what direction you are walking: east, west, north, or south. You can look at a compass to find out which way you're going. Or you can tell from where the sun is sitting in the sky. (The sun rises in the east, shines in the south, and sets in the west.) God will walk with you in any direction you walk.

October 10

Fire Safety

Royal Words

King Nebuchadnezzar leaped to his feet. He was so
amazed he asked his advisers, "Didn't we tie three men
up? Didn't we throw three men into the fire?"
"Yes, we did," they replied.

DANIEL 3:24

Princess Thoughts

Three men refused to worship a statue of King Nebuchadnezzar. These
three men worshiped only God. So soldiers threw the men into a very hot
fire. Then the king jumped up with excitement because he saw something
strange. He asked the soldiers if they threw three men in the fire.

A Prayer for the King

Father King, you are the only one for people to worship.
Help me to worship you.

Princess in Action

Practice fire safety rules, such as stay low and go, go, go! That means
to get low because it is easier to breathe if you stay close to the ground
or floor. So crouch down and crawl. Go means to go outside
and get away from the fire.

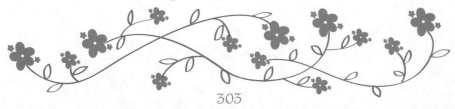

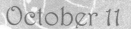

Fire Protection

Royal Words

The king said, "Look! I see four men walking around in the fire. They aren't tied up. And the fire hasn't even harmed them. The fourth man looks like a son of the gods."

DANIEL 3:25

Princess Thoughts

Soldiers threw three men into the fire, but King Nebuchadnezzar saw four men. People think the king saw God walking in the flames. God did not let the men burn. When the men came out of the fire, their hair did not even smell like smoke. This miracle showed the king that the men knew the one true God.

A Prayer for the King

Father King, protect me all the days of my life just like you protected the three men in the fire.

Princess in Action

Look for things in your house that will protect you from being burned. Look for fire extinguishers, smoke detectors, and pot holders. Talk with your mom or dad about how these things keep you safe.

October 12

A Bad Choice

Royal Words

The LORD God said to Adam, "You listened to your wife. You
ate the fruit of the tree that I commanded you about. I said,
'You must not eat its fruit.' So I am putting a curse on the
ground because of what you did. All the days of your life you
will have to work hard to get food from the ground."

GENESIS 3:17

Princess Thoughts

Oh no! God told Adam and Eve not to eat fruit from one tree.
But they did not follow God's rule. Adam and Eve made a bad choice
and ate the fruit. God knows what is good for us.
We should stay away from the things God says are bad.

A Prayer for the King

Dear Lord God, help me to follow your rules.

Princess in Action

Play a game to remember to make good choices. Put a sign with a smiley
face on one side of a room. Then put a sign with a sad face on the other
side of the room. Let your mom or dad call out an action (hitting a
friend, reading the Bible, or having a temper tantrum). If it's a good
action, run to the smiley face. If it's a bad action, run to the sad face.

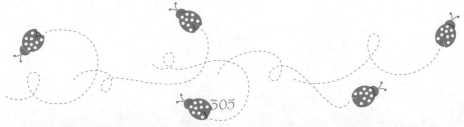

A Good Grip

Royal Words

God's law is in their hearts. Their feet do not slip.

PSALM 37:31

Princess Thoughts

Today's verse talks about people who follow God and learn God's words from the Bible. People who follow God choose to do good things instead of bad things. God's princess loves the Lord and follows what he teaches in the Bible.

A Prayer for the King

Father King, help me to learn your words by heart. Keep me from disobeying you.

Princess in Action

Check the bottom of your shoes. These are the soles. Some shoes have smooth soles, and it's easy to slip when wearing them. Other shoes have grooves or even spikes that grip the ground and keep a person from slipping. The Bible keeps you from slipping as you walk with God.

Energy Food

Royal Words

Those who trust in the LORD will receive new strength.
They will fly as high as eagles. They will run and not
get tired. They will walk and not grow weak.

ISAIAH 40:31

Princess Thoughts

God can help people when they think they are too tired to move.
God makes people strong and gives them energy.

A Prayer for the King

Father King, thanks for giving me energy. Help me to continue
trying when I feel tired.

Princess in Action

Eat some energy food. Some foods that give people
energy are tomatoes, oranges, blueberries, granola,
oatmeal, sweet potatoes, and nuts. Then pray to God
for help. He'll give you energy.

Harvesttime

Royal Words
[God] sends rain in the fall and the spring. He promises us that the harvest will come at the same time each year.
JEREMIAH 5:24

Princess Thoughts
The harvesttime is when fruits are ready to pick. All fruits need sunshine, time, and water to grow. God made the seasons, and every year apples ripen in the fall. Wow!

A Prayer for the King
Dear God, thanks for creating seasons and for sending rain to help plants grow.

Princess in Action
Go to an orchard to pick ripe fruits.
Or go to the store to find ripe fruits to buy.

October 16

Like a Good Tree

Royal Words

[The one who obeys God] is like a tree that is planted near a stream of water. It always bears its fruit at the right time. Its leaves don't dry up. Everything godly people do turns out well.

PSALM 1:3

Princess Thoughts

A good fruit tree grows strong and produces lots of fruit. The Bible says that people can be like a good tree. But people don't produce apples, peaches, or bananas. People produce good deeds. These good deeds make other people feel good and bring smiles to their faces.

A Prayer for the King

Father King, help me to make good choices that help people and bring smiles.

Princess in Action

Make fruit salad, and talk about how the fruit helps you grow. Then choose to do a good deed, like cleaning the table after dinner.

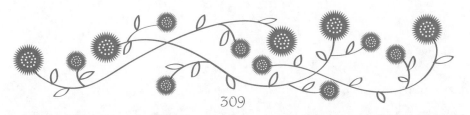

October 17

Seeds and Fruits

Royal Words

Every good tree bears good fruit. But
a bad tree bears bad fruit.
MATTHEW 7:17

Princess Thoughts

A crab apple tree grows only sour crab apples.
A pear tree grows only sweet pears. God used trees
to remind us to be full of good things. People full of love
give love to others. People full of anger yell and hurt
other people.

A Prayer for the King

Father God, help me to be full of love and to
forgive any hurt so I will be a person who gives
love to others.

Princess in Action

Have your mom or dad print pictures of seeds and
the fruits they become. Use the pictures to make a
game of matching the seeds to the fruit that grows
from the seed.

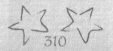

310

Beautiful Trees

Royal Words

Let the fields and everything in them be glad. Then
all of the trees in the forest will sing with joy.

PSALM 96:12

Princess Thoughts

The trees God made lift their limbs and trunks to the sky in praise.
When the wind blows through the trees, it sounds like they're
clapping their hands for God.

A Prayer for the King

Father King, thanks for all the trees you made, the fruit they grow,
and the shade they give.

Princess in Action

Take a tree walk and gather leaves that have fallen to the ground.
Look at the beauty of the trees, and praise God for each tree.
Listen to the sounds of leaves rustling in the wind.

Special Fruits

Royal Words

The fruit the Holy Spirit produces is love, joy and peace. It is being patient, kind and good. It is being faithful and gentle and having control of oneself.

GALATIANS 5:22-23

Princess Thoughts

The Bible tells us about special types of fruit. They are called the fruits of the Spirit. These fruits of the Spirit are all good things that we can have, like patience, joy, and love. The Holy Spirit helps God's followers to have more of these special fruits in their lives.

A Prayer for the King

Lord God, thanks for your Holy Spirit. Help me to have the fruits of the Spirit in my life.

Princess in Action

With your mom or dad, cut out paper fruit shapes. On each shape, write a name of one of the fruits of the Spirit from today's verse. Talk about each fruit and how you can help each one grow in your life. Practice using one of the fruits, like being patient when you need help or want something.

October 20

Pleasing God

Royal Words

We pray that you will lead a life that is worthy of the Lord. We pray that you will please him in every way. So we want you to bear fruit in every good thing you do. We want you to grow to know God better.

COLOSSIANS 1:10

Princess Thoughts

These words in the Bible are a prayer for you, God's princess. God wants you to bear fruit to please him. That means God wants you to do good things for him. God especially wants you to get to know him better. You learn about God and get to know him as you read the Bible and pray.

A Prayer for the King

Father King, help me to please you, to know you, and to bear fruit for you.

Princess in Action

Make a chart to track how you're bearing the fruits of the Spirit (see yesterday's verse). List fruits of the Spirit (love, joy, peace, patience, kindness, goodness, faithfulness, gentleness, self-control). Put a sticker on the chart each time you use a fruit of the Spirit. (For example, if you give your mom or dad a hug, you are using love.) See how fast you can fill the chart. A full chart shows that you are pleasing God with your great actions.

A Tender Princess

Royal Words

Be kind and tender to one another. Forgive each other, just as God forgave you because of what Christ has done.
EPHESIANS 4:32

Princess Thoughts

The Bible tells us how we should treat other people. We should be kind and tender to one another. The word *tender* means to be softhearted and gentle. When you have a cut, your mom gently cleans it and puts on a bandage. That's tender, loving care. God also wants us to forgive others when they hurt us. Forgiving others keeps our hearts soft and tender.

A Prayer for the King

Father King, keep my heart soft. Help me to be gentle.

Princess in Action

Touch a stuffed animal or a blanket. See how soft it is? God wants you to be a princess with a soft heart that forgives easily. When you feel angry or hurt, stop and forgive the person who hurt you.

October 22

Walking on Water

Royal Words

"Come," Jesus said. So Peter got out of the boat.
He walked on the water toward Jesus.

MATTHEW 14:29

Princess Thoughts

Jesus walked on water. He told Peter to come to him. So Peter got
out of the boat and walked on the water! Wow! It was a miracle.
Jesus can do anything!

A Prayer for the King

Lord Jesus, you are great and wonderful. Help me to do
whatever you ask.

Princess in Action

Place a blue towel or sheet on the floor. Step on it, and chat about
Peter and Jesus walking on water. Jump over the towel or sheet
like you're jumping over water.

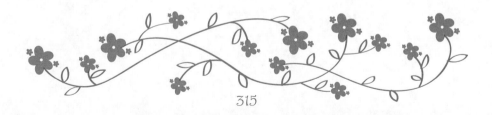

Jumping and Praising God

Royal Words

[The lame man] jumped to his feet and began to walk. He went with Peter and John into the temple courtyards. He walked and jumped and praised God.

ACTS 3:8

Princess Thoughts

People who are lame cannot use their legs to walk or jump. Peter asked God to heal a lame man. God healed the man! The man was able to jump and walk. He praised God for healing him.

A Prayer for the King

Father King, thank you for legs that run and jump. Thanks for healing people who cannot walk.

Princess in Action

Have a jumping praise party. Put some music on. Praise God while you jump as high as you can.

Training for a Race

Royal Words

I train my body and bring it under control. Then after I have preached to others, I myself will not break the rules and fail to win the prize.

1 Corinthians 9:27

Princess Thoughts

An athlete works hard and practices to develop strong leg muscles. A runner also learns to control his or her body and follows rules, like eating healthy, running without pushing someone down, and wearing good running shoes.

A Prayer for the King

Father King, thank you for my leg muscles. Help me to build strong muscles.

Princess in Action

Get ready to go for a run around your yard. Stretch your legs before you run. Walk a little to warm up your muscles. Drink some water before and after you run. Water helps your body not get too hot or too cold, and it keeps your heart pumping well. Have fun running!

October 25

You Are Important

Royal Words

In fact, [God] even counts every hair on your head! So
don't be afraid. You are worth more than many sparrows.

Luke 12:7

Princess Thoughts

You are worth more than birds in the sky! God made all kinds
of birds, and he likes them. He sees them flap their wings,
and he hears them tweet. You are more important to God
than birds. You are very special to God.

A Prayer for the King

Father King, I am thankful that I am important to you.

Princess in Action

Walk around your house and touch things that are
special to you. You might have a special toy or blanket.
Then think about how your family is even more special
than your toys and other things. You can put a sticker on
their hands to show they are special. Put a sticker on
your hand because you are special to Jesus.

Be Brave!

Royal Words
Right away Jesus called out to them, "Be brave! It is I. Don't be afraid."

MATTHEW 14:27

Princess Thoughts
The friends of Jesus sat in a boat on a lake and thought they saw a ghost. They had never seen anyone walk on water. But it was Jesus. He walked on the water to reach his friends. Jesus told his friends not to be afraid.

A Prayer for the King
Lord Jesus, help me to be brave. Help me to not be afraid when I see something I don't understand.

Princess in Action
At this time of year, people dress up in costumes and masks. Some masks look scary, but we don't need to feel afraid. Jesus is with us. Put pictures of things that scare you on index cards. Then place them around the floor. For each one, ask Jesus to help you be brave. Then jump over the pictures to leap over the fears.

Saved from Fear

Royal Words

I looked to the Lord, and he answered me. He saved me from everything I was afraid of.

Psalm 34:4

Princess Thoughts

God hears us when we cry because we are afraid. He helps us when something scares us.

A Prayer for the King

Father King, help me to be brave and trust you to help me when I am afraid.

Princess in Action

Have your mom or dad write today's verse on an index card. You can draw a smiley face and a heart on it. Put it under your pillow. When you lie down to sleep you can touch the card and remember that Jesus will help you when you feel afraid.

Dancing with Joy

Royal Words

Aaron's sister Miriam was a prophet. She took a
tambourine in her hand. All the women followed
her. They played tambourines and danced.

Exodus 15:20

Princess Thoughts

Miriam felt so happy because God rescued her and her people from
slavery and a mean ruler. Miriam and her friends danced and
played music with their tambourines.

A Prayer for the King

Father God, help me to dance with joy about all the great
things you do for me.

Princess in Action

Have a dance party with your family or friends. Play music and
ring bells. Shout out what God has done for you.

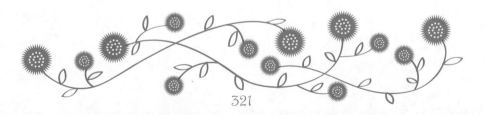

October 29

Thankful Dancing

Royal Words

David was wearing a sacred linen apron. He danced in the sight of the LORD with all his might.

2 SAMUEL 6:14

Princess Thoughts

King David danced and God saw him. David was happy because he and his soldiers had won a battle and brought back something special. It was a large gold box called the Ark of the Covenant. This special box contained important items to help God's people.

A Prayer for the King

Father King, my Bible is an important reminder of you. Help me to care for it and dance with joy that I have one.

Princess in Action

Place your Bible somewhere special. Then dance with joy because you have a Bible that contains words from God.

October 30

Praise Dance

Royal Words

Let them praise [God's] name with dancing. Let them
make music to him with harps and tambourines.

PSALM 149:3

Princess Thoughts

God has many names, like Savior, Creator, Lord, Prince of Peace,
King, and Father. Each name reminds us of what God can do.
God's names give us more reasons to praise him.

A Prayer for the King

Father King, you are almighty God and Creator.
I will praise you.

Princess in Action

Have a dance parade. Call out different names for God,
like Creator and mighty God, and cheer for God.

Joy and Truth

Royal Words

Love is not happy with evil. But it is full
of joy when the truth is spoken.

1 CORINTHIANS 13:6

Princess Thoughts

Today's verse is part of a lesson in the Bible about love. It
reminds us not to be happy when someone is hurt or when
something bad happens. God wants us to feel joy when we
hear the truth, especially truth about Jesus. He wants us to
always tell the truth too.

A Prayer for the King

Father King, thank you for teaching me your truths in the Bible.
Help me to always tell the truth.

Princess in Action

Talk about truths you know about God. (He is wonderful. He
can do anything. He always loves you.) Leap high for joy at
each truth. Be sure to tell the truth today, even if it means
telling that you did something wrong.
That's called confessing.

November

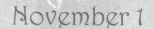

God's Seal of Approval

Royal Words

When you believed, [God] marked you with a seal.
The seal is the Holy Spirit that he promised.

<small>EPHESIANS 1:13</small>

Princess Thoughts

Wow! If you asked Jesus to forgive your sins, he saved you and marked you with a seal. This type of seal is like a stamp. It's not something people see, though. It's inside your heart. The seal is a sign that you are a follower of God.

A Prayer for the King

Lord Jesus, thank you for putting a seal on your followers.

Princess in Action

God puts his seal, like a stamp, on you when you believe in Jesus. Find, buy, or make a stamp of a crown or heart. You can make a stamp out of a potato or art foam. Stamp the crown or heart on paper, and remember that Jesus loves you and puts a seal on your heart.

November 2

Approved

Royal Words
God the Father has put his seal of approval on [Jesus].
John 6:27

Princess Thoughts
A seal of approval means that something or someone is accepted and meets the requirements to belong. God the Father put his seal of approval on Jesus. God also accepts you and loves you, his princess. That's a great gift.

A Prayer for the King
King Jesus, thank you for your promise to love me forever.

Princess in Action
Stamp your hand with the seal you made yesterday. Cut out paper hearts and stamp them with the seal. Give them to people to show that you love them.

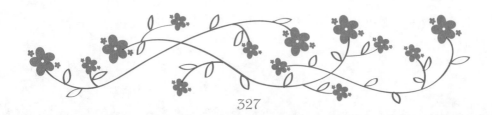

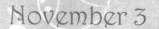

Promises

Royal Words

[King Xerxes said to Queen Esther,] "Now write another order in my name. Do it for the benefit of the Jews. Do what seems best to you. Stamp the order with my royal seal. Nothing that is written in my name and stamped with my seal can ever be changed."

ESTHER 8:8

Princess Thoughts

In Bible times, a king's stamp sealed an order. That meant nothing could change the order. A king named Xerxes promised to save Queen Esther's people. His workers stamped letters that told people about the promise. The letters were sent to people in all the cities the king ruled.

A Prayer for the King

Lord Jesus, thank you for keeping your promise to save everyone who believes in you.

Princess in Action

Draw crosses on some sheets of paper. Then stamp the papers with your seal from the November 1 devotion. Give the papers to friends to share God's promise that he died for them and will save them.

November 4

God Made Today

Royal Words
This is the day the LORD has made. We will
rejoice and be glad in it.
PSALM 118:24, NLT

Princess Thoughts
God made today. He makes every day. He made yesterday,
and he will make tomorrow. God wants us to be happy he
made today. We should praise him.

A Prayer for the King
Father King, thanks for making today. Help me to
be happy today.

Princess in Action
Look at a calendar and see what day it is. Talk about the
days of the week and how each morning is a new day.
Be thankful for today.

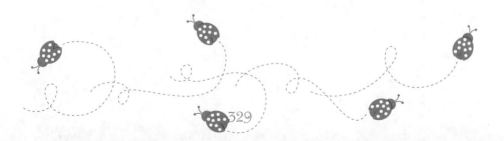

God Hears

Royal Words
If we know that God hears what we ask
for, we know that we have it.
1 John 5:15

Princess Thoughts
God wants us to trust that he will answer our prayers.
He always hears us. Answers to prayer are gifts from
God. His answers are not always what we expect.
We can still trust that God knows what is best for us.

A Prayer for the King
Father King, thanks for listening to me and
answering my prayers.

Princess in Action
Look at the prayer answers in the diary you started on
September 1. Stamp the prayers answered with the
princess seal you made on November 1. Praise God
for each answer.

Always Thankful

Royal Words

Remember to thank [God] for what he's done. People
have praised him with their songs.

JOB 36:24

Princess Thoughts

Job had a very bad day. Poor Job! But Job still told his friends to
thank God. He trusted that God would take care of him even
when he had huge problems. And God did!

A Prayer for the King

Father King, help me to thank you even when
I have a bad day.

Princess in Action

Stamp your hand with your princess seal that you made on
November 1. Use this stamp as a reminder to trust God and
to thank him tonight before you go to sleep. Thank him even
if you had a bad day.

Giving Thanks Each Day

Royal Words
Give thanks no matter what happens. God wants you
to thank him because you believe in Christ Jesus.
1 THESSALONIANS 5:18

Princess Thoughts
God wants his people to be thankful no matter what
happens. God wants us to remember to be thankful that
he sent Jesus. We may have problems now, but we know
we will have only happy days in heaven.

A Prayer for the King
Father God, thank you for sending your Son, Jesus.

Princess in Action
Each morning thank God for the day no matter what
happens. Put a stamp on your hand to remember
to thank God all day.

November 8

Tongues That Speak

Royal Words

A tongue that brings healing is like a tree of life. But
a tongue that tells lies produces a broken spirit.

PROVERBS 15:4

Princess Thoughts

Our tongue helps us to speak. But we can choose which
words to say. Helpful words can make people feel better.
Words that lie hurt people.

A Prayer for the King

Father King, help me to use my tongue to say sweet
words and to tell the truth.

Princess in Action

Practice using your tongue to talk. Try some tongue twisters like,
"Pretty precious princesses pick purple plants."

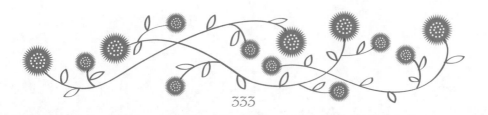

November 9

Laughter

Royal Words

Our mouths were filled with laughter. Our tongues
sang with joy. Then the people of other nations
said, "The LORD has done great things for them."
PSALM 126:2

Princess Thoughts

People laugh when they feel joyful or happy. When all
God's people laughed together, other people noticed and
saw that God had blessed the Israelites. Going to church
and being with other believers should be times for us
to laugh and sing.

A Prayer for the King

Lord God, fill me with laughter and joy.

Princess in Action

Tell jokes or make funny faces to see if you can make
people smile and laugh. Tell them about what God has
done for you, and smile about that too.

A Healed Tongue

Royal Words

Jesus took the man to one side, away from the crowd. He put his fingers into the man's ears. Then he spit and touched the man's tongue. . . . The man's ears were opened. His tongue was freed up, and he began to speak clearly.

MARK 7:33, 35

Princess Thoughts

A deaf man who could not hear or talk went to Jesus for help. Jesus healed the man. The man started to speak clearly. What a miracle!

A Prayer for the King

Father King, thank you for my ears and tongue. Help me to speak clearly so people will understand.

Princess in Action

Try using no words to tell your mom or dad what you need.
You can point or make signs.
Can your parent understand you?

November 11

Helping Your Church

Royal Words

The Spirit of the LORD spoke through me.
I spoke his word with my tongue.

2 SAMUEL 23:2

Princess Thoughts

The prophet Samuel listened to God and then shared
the words God spoke to him. Samuel used words to share
news about God. Samuel was just a young boy, but he
helped at church.

A Prayer for the King

Dear God, help me to listen when I pray. Help me
to share my faith.

Princess in Action

You are young, but you can be a good helper. Help your
Sunday school teacher. Walk around your church with
an adult, and pick up litter to keep the church clean.

November 12

Fiery Tongues

Royal Words

They saw something that looked like tongues of fire.
The flames separated and settled on each of them.

ACTS 2:3

Princess Thoughts

The tongues in today's Bible verse were very special tongues.
These tongues looked like flames of fire, but they didn't burn
anything up. The flames came from God's Holy Spirit and
rested on people praying. Each person became filled with
power from the Holy Spirit. They even spoke in languages
they had never spoken before. This happened on the Day of
Pentecost when the church began.

A Prayer for the King

Father King, thank you for sending us the Holy Spirit.

Princess in Action

Make a princess crown. Cut out and color a paper flame, and
put it on your crown. Wear it as a reminder that God sends
his Holy Spirit to help you, his princess.

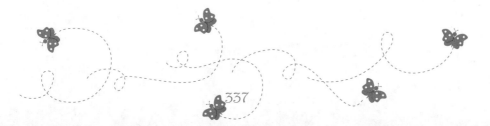

Steering Words

Royal Words

How about ships? They are very big. They are driven along by strong winds. But they are steered by a very small rudder. It makes them go where the captain wants to go.

James 3:4

Princess Thoughts

A rudder is a small piece on a boat that looks like a flat tail. A rudder helps steer a boat. The words in today's Bible verse are about how the tongue is also small but steers what we say and do. Our tongues can cause lots of trouble if we say the wrong things.

A Prayer for the King

Father God, help me to use my tongue for good and not to cause trouble with my words.

Princess in Action

Steer one of your toy cars through an obstacle course. Then use your tongue to say good things. Steer away from lying or whining. Think before you talk.

Thankful Tongues

Royal Words

"Sir, I hope you will continue to be kind to me," Ruth said.
"You have comforted me. You have spoken kindly to me. And
I'm not even as important as one of your female servants!"
RUTH 2:13

Princess Thoughts

Ruth thanked Boaz, a great leader who owned a big
farm. He spoke kindly to her and treated her like a
princess. A princess remembers to thank people,
especially when they are kind. Later Boaz married Ruth.

A Prayer for the King

Father King, help me to thank people who are kind.

Princess in Action

Take care of your tongue. Remember to brush your
tongue when you brush your teeth. Brushing removes
germs from your tongue. Use your clean tongue to say
thankful words to people today.

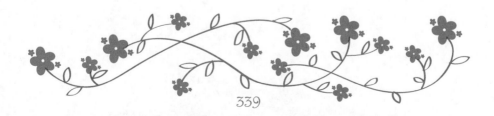

November 15

Truth and Fiction

Royal Words

We will speak the truth in love. We will grow up
into Christ in every way. He is the Head.
EPHESIANS 4:15

Princess Thoughts

Today's verse tells us that love and truth go together. Lies
hurt people. Truth makes us happy even when we tell the
truth about doing something wrong.

A Prayer for the King

Father King, help me to always tell the truth.

Princess in Action

Look at storybooks and books of facts (nonfiction).
Storybooks tell a story that is made up. Books of facts share
facts that are real and true. Talk about the difference between
the truth, lies, and make-believe.

November 16

Right Answers

Royal Words
Joy is found in giving the right answer. And how
good is a word spoken at the right time!
PROVERBS 15:23

Princess Thoughts
Words are important. We can choose to say good things
to help people feel better. The Bible says that we will be
joyful when we choose to encourage people or cheer
people up with our words.

A Prayer for the King
Father King, please help me give good answers.

Princess in Action
Practice giving good answers. Ask your mom or dad to
give you examples of times you can help someone with
your words (someone is hurt, someone is sad). Then tell
your mom or dad what you would say.

Joyful Tongue

Royal Words
My heart is glad. Joy is on my tongue. My
body also will be secure.
PSALM 16:9

Princess Thoughts
A happy person shouts for joy or laughs and tells
people why she is happy. A happy person feels good
from head to toe.

A Prayer for the King
Father God, thank you for making my heart happy
and giving me laughter.

Princess in Action
Point to each part of your body, and thank God
for each part.

Bow to the King

Royal Words

When the name of Jesus is spoken, everyone's knee
will bow to worship him. Every knee in heaven and on
earth and under the earth will bow to worship him.

PHILIPPIANS 2:10

Princess Thoughts

People bow to a king to honor the king. Someday everyone
will bow to Jesus. He is the King of kings.

A Prayer for the King

Lord Jesus, you are the King of kings. Help me to remember
that your name is special.

Princess in Action

Practice bows and curtsies. Bow your head when you
hear the name of Jesus.

God Listens

Royal Words

There is one thing we can be sure of when we come to God in prayer. If we ask anything in keeping with what he wants, he hears us.

1 JOHN 5:14

Princess Thoughts

God tells us that he always listens to our prayers. He pays attention to prayers that are good and follow his rules. That means we should pray for things that will not hurt other people.

A Prayer for the King

Father God, thank you for always listening to my prayers.

Princess in Action

Cut out pictures of things to talk to God about. Put them in a bowl. Take out one at a time and talk to God about it. That's another way to pray.

Praying Together

Royal Words

[Jesus said,] "Here is what I tell you. Suppose two of you on earth agree about anything you ask for. My Father in heaven will do it for you."

MATTHEW 18:19

Princess Thoughts

Jesus said that if people agree and pray together for the same prayer request, God will answer. God can do anything. He can answer our biggest prayers.

A Prayer for the King

Father God, thank you for answering my prayers.

Princess in Action

With your family or friends, talk about some things you want to ask God to do. Agree on what to pray about with them. Then pray together for that need.

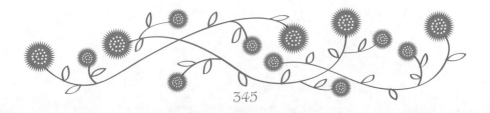

Chain of Thanksgiving

Royal Words
I will praise the LORD. I won't forget anything he does for me.
PSALM 103:2

Princess Thoughts
God wants us to praise him and to remember what he
has done for us. Remembering what God has done helps
us to trust God more.

A Prayer for the King
Father King, thanks for all you do. Help me to remember
all you have given me.

Princess in Action
Start a thanksgiving chain. Cut strips of paper. On each
one draw or have a grown-up write something God did
for you. Make the strips into a chain by looping one into
the next and closing each strip with tape, staples, or
glue. Watch the chain grow as you think of more things
God has done. On Thanksgiving Day, use your
thanksgiving chain as a decoration.

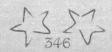

Jesus Spoke the Truth

Royal Words

[Jesus'] disciples later remembered what he had said. That was after he had been raised from the dead. Then they believed the Scriptures. They also believed the words that Jesus had spoken.

JOHN 2:22

Princess Thoughts

Why did the disciples of Jesus believe? The disciples believed because Jesus said he would rise from the dead, and then he did rise from the dead. Jesus kept his promise. Jesus always keeps his promises.

A Prayer for the King

Lord Jesus, I believe in you. Help me to keep my promises.

Princess in Action

Cut the corner of an envelope to make a bookmark. Stamp it with a seal, or add a sticker. Slip your bookmark over the corner of a page in your Bible or this book to find the page again. When you see your bookmark, remember that Jesus keeps his promises.

347

Thanking God for People

Royal Words
I thank my God every time I remember you.
PHILIPPIANS 1:3

Princess Thoughts
Paul told his friends that every time he thought of them, he thanked God. It's so good to thank God for the people we love.

A Prayer for the King
Father King, thanks for my family and friends.

Princess in Action
Let an adult tape a big piece of paper or poster board to your wall. Write in names or draw pictures of people to pray for on the paper. This is your prayer wall. Pray and thank God for the people you love.

November 24

God Is Good

Royal Words

Give thanks to the LORD, because he is good.
His faithful love continues forever.

PSALM 136:1

Princess Thoughts

The Bible has special songs called psalms. The psalm above tells us to thank God. God is good, and he always loves us. Thanksgiving is a special day to thank God. The people who settled this country started Thanksgiving in the United States.

A Prayer for the King

Father God, thank you for all you give me. Thanks for my country and for the people who lead us. Please give our leaders wisdom.

Princess in Action

Fold a piece of paper. Put the side of your hand with the little finger beside the fold. Let your mom or dad trace your hand. Help cut the paper hand, but don't cut the fold. Your paper hand can open and close. On each paper finger, write a reason to thank God. Inside the hand, draw a picture of your Thanksgiving Day. Stamp the paper hand with your princess seal that you made on November 1.

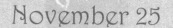

Songs of Thanks

Royal Words

On that day large numbers of sacrifices were offered. The people were glad because God had given them great joy. The women and children were also very happy. The joyful sound in Jerusalem could be heard far away.

NEHEMIAH 12:43

Princess Thoughts

In today's Bible verse, the Israelites were celebrating the good things God had done for them. It was a special day of thanksgiving for them. The Israelites were very happy. Their singing could be heard from far away.

A Prayer for the King

Father King, thanks for giving me reasons to laugh and sing.

Princess in Action

Sing with your family or friends. Sing songs to thank God for his love. Sing loud and play music.

Neighborhood Thanks Walk

Royal Words

I will give you thanks in the whole community. Among all of your people I will praise you.

PSALM 35:18

Princess Thoughts

When a person smiles, laughs, and gives thanks, it helps other people feel happy too. God wants everyone around you to see you praising him.

A Prayer for the King

Father King, thanks for giving me friends in my neighborhood and at church so we can praise you together.

Princess in Action

Take a thanks walk. Make a sign to praise Jesus. Walk around your neighborhood holding the sign.
Sing songs about Jesus as you walk.

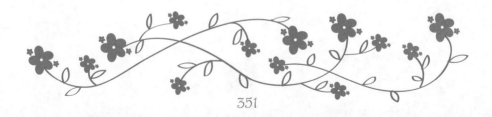

Princess Tongues

Royal Words

Keep your tongues from speaking evil.
Keep your lips from telling lies.

PSALM 34:13

Princess Thoughts

It's important to tell the truth and not to tell lies or say mean words. A princess always tells the truth.

A Prayer for the King

Father King, help me to always tell the truth.

Princess in Action

Taste sweet, sour, and bitter foods. You can tell the difference because of taste buds in your tongue. Lies are bitter, and they hurt people. But telling the truth with love is like giving a sweet treat to people.

November 28

Sharing

Royal Words

Jesus directed the people to sit down on the grass. He took the five loaves and the two fish. He looked up to heaven and gave thanks. He broke the loaves into pieces. Then he gave them to the disciples. And the disciples gave them to the people.

MATTHEW 14:19

Princess Thoughts

Jesus took a little bread and thanked God the Father. Then a miracle happened! The five loaves of bread fed many people. It's important to thank God for all we have. God can use the things we have to do great things.

A Prayer for the King

Dear Lord, thank you for my family, friends, home, church, toys, and books.

Princess in Action

Look at the food in your kitchen. What can you make for your friends when they come over? Look at your toys. Which ones can you give your friends to play with when they come to your house?

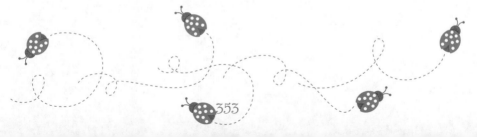

Communion

Royal Words
While they were eating, Jesus took bread. He
gave thanks and broke it. He handed it to his
disciples and said, "Take this and eat it."
MATTHEW 26:26

Princess Thoughts
Jesus ate a special supper with his friends. At the supper
he started what we call Communion or the Lord's
Supper. Jesus thanked God the Father for the bread.
Then he told his friends to eat the bread.

A Prayer for the King
Father King, thanks for sending Jesus and giving
us Communion.

Princess in Action
Talk about how your church celebrates Communion
or the Lord's Supper.

November 30

Jesus and Bread

Royal Words

[Jesus] joined [the two men] at the table. Then he took bread and gave thanks. He broke it and began to give it to them. Their eyes were opened, and they recognized him.

LUKE 24:30-31

Princess Thoughts

After Jesus rose from the dead, he walked with two of his followers for a long time. But they did not recognize him until he prayed for their bread and gave it to them.

A Prayer for the King

Lord Jesus, please help me to know you better and to recognize when you are talking to me.

Princess in Action

Help your mom or dad make bread or refrigerated rolls. Share the food with your family, and talk about Jesus as you eat.

December

Gifts for a Princess

Royal Words

Every good and perfect gift is from God. It comes
down from the Father. He created the heavenly lights.
He does not change like shadows that move.

JAMES 1:17

Princess Thoughts

God loves to bless his children with gifts. His gifts are always good
for us. Even the stars are gifts to enjoy. He made the stars that
twinkle in the sky for us. God never changes. He always loves us.

A Prayer for the King

Father King, thank you for all the gifts you give me. Thank you for
the stars and sunshine. Thank you for food, flowers, and friends.

Princess in Action

Find a box with a lid. Wrap the box with pretty paper. Wrap the
lid so you can put it on and take it off. Add a pretty bow. Write a
note or draw a picture to thank God for all the gifts he has given
you. Put your note in the gift box.

Gifts from God's Holy Spirit

Royal Words

There are different kinds of gifts. But they
are all given by the same Spirit.

1 CORINTHIANS 12:4

Princess Thoughts

You are not the same as anyone else. There is no other person
exactly like you. The Holy Spirit of God gives us each special
talents or abilities. These are called spiritual gifts. The Holy
Spirit decides what spiritual gifts to give each person.

A Prayer for the King

Holy Spirit, thanks for choosing what spiritual gifts are best for me.
Help me to use my spiritual gifts wisely.

Princess in Action

Think of the spiritual gifts you have, such as encouraging your friends,
being a cheerful giver, or being a great helper in the kitchen.
(Your mom or dad can read aloud 1 Corinthians 12 for more ideas.)
On a piece of paper, trace around a Christmas cookie cutter. With a
grown-up's help, cut out the shape. Then write or draw your spiritual
gift on the cutout. Use it as a Christmas ornament.

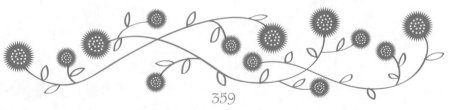

Asking God for Gifts

Royal Words

Even though you are evil, you know how to give good gifts
to your children. How much more will your Father who
is in heaven give good gifts to those who ask him!

MATTHEW 7:11

Princess Thoughts

Parents are not perfect like God, but parents give their children
good gifts. God gives the best gifts. We can ask God for anything.
He will give us gifts that are good for us.

A Prayer for the King

Father King, thank you for giving me the best gifts that are good
for me.

Princess in Action

God likes giving you gifts, but he also knows what you really need.
Draw a picture of what you want. Put your picture in the gift box
you made on December 1. Trust that God will give you what
you've asked for or something that's even better for you.

December 4

Rebekah's Gifts

Royal Words

[Abraham's servant] brought out gold and silver jewelry. He brought out articles of clothing. He gave all of it to Rebekah. He also gave expensive gifts to her brother and her mother.

GENESIS 24:53

Princess Thoughts

Rebekah said yes to marrying Isaac, the son of Abraham. So Abraham's servant gave Rebekah pretty clothes and jewelry. After Rebekah married Isaac, they had children. Then those children had children. And their children had children. After many, many years and many, many children, Jesus was born.

A Prayer for the King

Father God, thank you for my clothes and jewelry. Thank you most of all for giving me Jesus.

Princess in Action

Christmas is coming! Christmas is a time to give gifts to other people. Write a list of gifts you want to give your mommy, daddy, and other people. Write a note of something you will do for Jesus (like praying each day). Put it in the gift box you made on December 1.

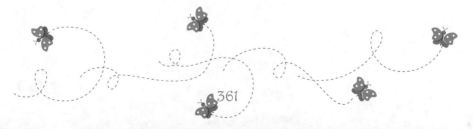

You Are a Gift!

Royal Words
Children are a gift from the LORD.
They are a reward from him.
PSALM 127:3

Princess Thoughts
Children are gifts to their parents. Every princess or prince is very special to God. He chose your mommy and daddy just for you. He gave you to your parents as a precious gift.

A Prayer for the King
Father King, thanks for making me and for giving me to my mommy and daddy.

Princess in Action
Put a bow on your head. Let your mom or dad take a photo of you with the bow. You're a gift! Your love is also a gift. Put your photo in the gift box you made on December 1. You're a gift to God, too!

December 6

Toys for the Poor

Royal Words

He said, "Cornelius, God has heard your prayer. He has remembered your gifts to poor people."

ACTS 10:31

Princess Thoughts

Cornelius believed in God and prayed to him every day. Cornelius shared his love with people and gave them gifts. God saw Cornelius and blessed him. God sent a special friend of Jesus, Peter, to give a message to Cornelius and his friends. That day many people became Christians.

A Prayer for the King

Father King, thanks for teaching me about Jesus and about the gift of being a Christian. Help me to share your love with other people.

Princess in Action

Help pick out a toy for a needy child. You might get a child's name from an angel tree program. Or you might put the toy in a box for a group that collects toys for children. That's one way to share God's love with others.

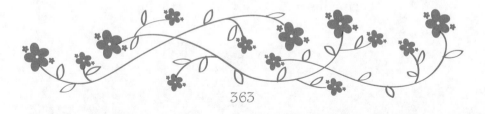

I Am a Gift to God

Royal Words

The Lord came and stood there. He called out, just as he had done the other times. He said, "Samuel! Samuel!"
Then Samuel replied, "Speak. I'm listening."

1 Samuel 3:10

Princess Thoughts

God called out to Samuel, a young boy, in the middle of the night. Samuel thought the priest called him and ran to obey. But the priest did not call Samuel. The priest told Samuel to answer God. So God called Samuel again, and Samuel said, "I'm listening." Samuel became a great priest for God's people. He listened and did all God told him. God wants his people to listen and obey.

A Prayer for the King

Father King, your princess is listening.
Please speak and tell me what to do.

Princess in Action

God wants you! Draw a big heart or Christmas tree. Draw on it things you will do for God, like listening, obeying his rules, or giving toys to the poor.

December 8

Princess Clothes

Royal Words

When it snows, [the godly woman]'s not afraid for her
family. All of them are dressed in the finest clothes.

PROVERBS 31:21

Princess Thoughts

Good mothers provide clothes for their families and care for
the clothes by washing them. Some mothers, like the one in
today's verse, even make beautiful clothes. The clothes keep a
princess warm when it's cold.

A Prayer for the King

Father King, thank you for my pretty clothes.

Princess in Action

Look at your clothes and find out about the fabrics used to
make them. There may be knits, cotton, wool, or even silk.
Thank God and your mom for your clothes.

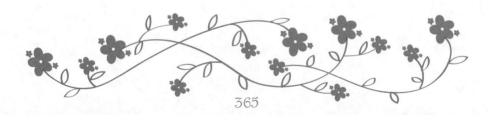

December 9

Christmas Cards

Royal Words

Everyone said good things about [Jesus]. They were
amazed at the gracious words they heard from his lips.
LUKE 4:22

Princess Thoughts

When Jesus lived on the earth, people said good things about
him. Jesus told people about God the Father. Jesus' words
amazed the people. They wondered how he could be so wise.
They did not understand that Jesus was God's Son.

A Prayer for the King

Lord Jesus, thank you for teaching me about
God the Father.

Princess in Action

Make Christmas cards with a Bible verse. Ask an adult to
help you write or print a verse such as Mark 1:1 or John
20:31. These verses help people know that Jesus is God the
Son. Give the cards to friends.

A Talking Donkey

Royal Words

The donkey saw the angel of the LORD. So it lay down under Balaam. That made [Balaam] angry. . . . Then the LORD opened the donkey's mouth. It said to Balaam, "What have I done to you?"

NUMBERS 22:27-28

Princess Thoughts

Balaam rode his donkey and kept getting mad. He wanted the donkey to walk between two walls. But the donkey saw an angel and would not budge. Balaam couldn't see the angel. Finally, God opened the mouth of the donkey, and the donkey spoke to Balaam. Then Balaam saw the angel.

A Prayer for the King

Father King, you are so great. You can even cause animals to talk. Thanks for using animals to teach us.

Princess in Action

Look at your family's nativity set. (If you don't have one, look up "nativity scene pictures" online.) Talk about how each animal helps people.

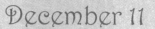

December 11

Lips That Invite People to Be Friends

Royal Words
Lord, guard my mouth. Keep watch over the door of my lips.
Psalm 141:3

Princess Thoughts
Today's verse is a prayer asking for God's help to not say hurtful words. Lips are like a door. Helpful and kind words invite people to open up and be a friend. Hurtful words are like slamming a door in someone's face to keep him or her away.

A Prayer for the King
Dear God, help guard my mouth. Help me to use my lips to say kind words that invite people to be my friends.

Princess in Action
Pass out sweet candy canes. Tell people how the upside-down cane forms a letter J for Jesus.

Pleasant Words

Royal Words

Lord, may the words of my mouth and the thoughts of my heart be pleasing in your eyes. You are my Rock and my Redeemer.

Psalm 19:14

Princess Thoughts

A princess wants to please her King. We please God with words of praise and words that share love. Calling God a Rock and Redeemer is praising him. God is solid like a rock. He saved (redeemed) you. Praise God for the things he has done!

A Prayer for the King

Father King, thank you for saving me. That's a great gift. Help me to share love and please you.

Princess in Action

Learn to care for your mouth. Brush your teeth and your tongue for fresh breath. Use lip balm to keep your lips soft when it's cold outside.

Creatures Praise God

Royal Words

I will praise the LORD with my mouth. Let every
creature praise his holy name for ever and ever.

PSALM 145:21

Princess Thoughts

God has always done great things. We can praise him every day,
especially as we prepare for Christmas. The animals that God
made also praise God with their noises.

A Prayer for the King

Father God, you are great and awesome.

Princess in Action

Say "Merry Christmas" to everyone you see, even your pets.

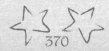

December 14

Many Languages

Royal Words

A crowd came together when they heard the sound.
They were bewildered because they each heard the
believers speaking in their own language.

ACTS 2:6

Princess Thoughts

People from different countries speak different languages. One day
during Bible times, the Holy Spirit gave people the ability to speak in
different languages. People felt puzzled on that day when they heard
a person speak a foreign language but heard the words in their own
language. So, if the person said, "Good day" in English, a person from
Germany would have heard "Guten Tag," and a person from Spain
would have heard "Buenos días." This ability to understand was a
special gift from the Holy Spirit.

A Prayer for the King

Father King, thank you for helping people of all languages
to understand your Word.

Princess in Action

Learn to say Merry Christmas in other languages. Try *Joyeux Noël*
in French, *Mele Kalikimaka* in Hawaiian, *Merry Keshmish* in
Navajo, *Feliz Natal* in Portuguese, or *Sung Tan Chuk Ha* in Korean.

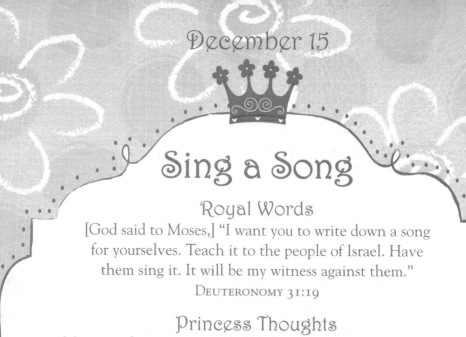

Sing a Song

Royal Words

[God said to Moses,] "I want you to write down a song for yourselves. Teach it to the people of Israel. Have them sing it. It will be my witness against them."

DEUTERONOMY 31:19

Princess Thoughts

Moses made up a song and told the Israelites to remember it. The song praised God and told about God caring for his people. It also told how the Israelites would turn away from God and how enemies would fight them. The song then told how God would stop the enemies. The song helped people to remember God's promises.

A Prayer for the King

Father King, let me remember all you do as I sing about you.

Princess in Action

Sing some Christmas carols. Talk about the words and how they remind you of what happened when Jesus came as a baby.

December 16

Angelic Voices

Royal Words

Suddenly a large group of angels from heaven
also appeared. They were praising God.

LUKE 2:13

Princess Thoughts

Angels filled the sky and sang praises to God. They sang about
peace on earth. They rejoiced when Jesus came.

A Prayer for the King

Lord God, thanks for music and songs that praise Jesus.

Princess in Action

Share the good news about Jesus. Go Christmas caroling
with your family. Knock on your neighbors' doors and
sing Christmas songs for them.

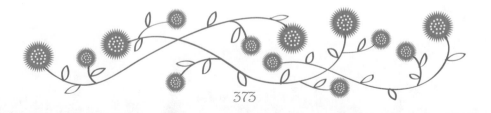

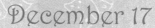

God's Words in Your Heart

Royal Words

It is pleasing when you keep [God's words] in your heart. Have all of them ready on your lips.

PROVERBS 22:18

Princess Thoughts

God wants you to know his words in the Bible. He wants you to be ready to share them with other people. When you have a problem, you can repeat the verses you know to help you.

A Prayer for the King

Father King, please help me to remember your words.

Princess in Action

Say a Bible verse that you know by heart. Talk about how those words can help you.

December 18

Oh, Christmas Tree

Royal Words

[God said,] "I will answer the prayers of my people. I will take good care of them. I will be like a green pine tree to them. All of the fruit they bear will come from me."

HOSEA 14:8

Princess Thoughts

God told us that he is like a green pine tree. We use pine trees as Christmas trees. All of the good things we do come from God.

A Prayer for the King

Father God, thanks for being like an evergreen tree. Let the Christmas tree remind me of you.

Princess in Action

Enjoy your Christmas tree. Turn off all the lights in the room except for the Christmas tree lights. The lights on the tree can help you remember to be a light for Jesus.

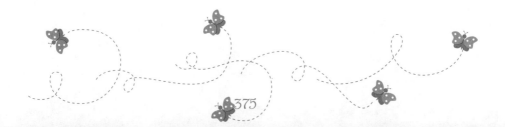

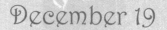

Gift of Life

Royal Words
When you sin, the pay you get is death. But
God gives you the gift of eternal life because
of what Christ Jesus our Lord has done.
ROMANS 6:23

Princess Thoughts
God gave you the gift of life when he made you in your mommy's
belly. God also gives you the gift of life forever in heaven.
God loved you from the very start, and he will always love you.
Your life is a precious gift. You are God's princess.

A Prayer for the King
Father King, thank you for giving us life on earth
and life forever in heaven.

Princess in Action
A wreath is a circle made of evergreens. As a circle, it is never
ending, like God's love. The fresh evergreen color is a reminder
that God's love is always alive. Hang a wreath on your door.
Add a heart as a reminder of God's love.

December 20

Family Photo

Royal Words

You are no longer strangers and outsiders. You are citizens together with God's people. You are members of God's family.

EPHESIANS 2:19

Princess Thoughts

If you asked Jesus to forgive your sins, you are part of a special family. You are in God's family. That's a very big family! Everyone who follows Jesus is part of God's family.

A Prayer for the King

Father King, thanks for inviting me to be a part of your family.

Princess in Action

Make one of your photos into a Christmas ornament. Put it on the Christmas tree. It can remind you that you are part of God's family and in his family tree.

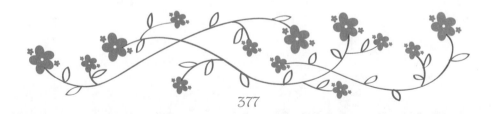

December 21

Bethlehem and the Jesse Tree

Royal Words

The LORD says, "Bethlehem, you might not be an important town in the nation of Judah. But out of you will come a ruler over Israel for me. His family line goes back to the early years of your nation. It goes all the way back to days of long ago."

MICAH 5:2

Princess Thoughts

Bethlehem became important because Jesus was born there. God told people this would happen hundreds of years before it did. Only God could know. He also knew all the people in the family of Jesus long before the night when Jesus came.

A Prayer for the King

Dear God, you know all things. Thanks for choosing to send Jesus.

Princess in Action

Make a Jesse Tree with your family. A Jesse Tree uses symbols all the way back to Adam and Eve to show the people in the family of Jesus. Your mom or dad can look on the Internet for the symbols to make.

Sharing Good News

Royal Words

The shepherds returned. They gave glory and praise to God.
Everything they had seen and heard was just as they had been told.

LUKE 2:20

Princess Thoughts

The shepherds found Jesus just where the angel told them to look.
They praised God! The shepherds shared the news about the
special baby with everyone they saw.

A Prayer for the King

Father King, help me to share the news of Jesus
with everyone I meet.

Princess in Action

Play a game. Let your mom or dad hide a baby Jesus figurine
(you can use a doll if you don't have one). See if you can find
him. Your parents can give clues about where the baby
Jesus is, just like the angel did.

Hit the Goal

Royal Words

We try our best to please [the Lord].

2 CORINTHIANS 5:9

Princess Thoughts

A princess wants to please the King. Every day a good goal is to do something to please God. This can be through praying, singing praise to God, saying kind words, or helping others.

A Prayer for the King

Father King, help me to please you.

Princess in Action

Play a game that has a goal, like soccer or hockey. Talk about how you have to aim at the goal to hit it. You also need to look to God to meet the goal of pleasing him.

December 24

News from an Angel

Royal Words

[The angel said to the shepherds,] "Today in the town of David a Savior has been born to you. He is Christ the Lord."

LUKE 2:11

Princess Thoughts

An angel surprised the shepherds at night as they watched their little lambs and sheep. The shepherds shook with fear. But the angel told them not to be afraid. The angel told the shepherds that Jesus had been born in the town of David, Bethlehem.

A Prayer for the King

Father King, thank you for angels who watch over us and share good news.

Princess in Action

If there's snow on the ground, bundle up and make snow angels outside. If there's no snow, make a flour or salt angel with an adult's help. Pour flour or salt in a cake pan. Use your hand, and press down to make an angel's body. Make a circle head with your thumb. Then swish your baby finger on one side to make a wing. Do the same on the other side.

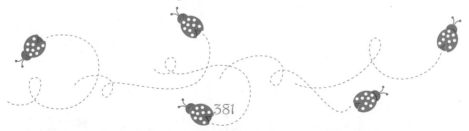

December 25

The Birthday Boy

Royal Words

[Mary] gave birth to her first baby. It was a boy. She
wrapped him in large strips of cloth. Then she placed him
in a manger. There was no room for them in the inn.

LUKE 2:7

Princess Thoughts

Mary gave birth to Jesus. Hooray! Jesus is the reason we
celebrate Christmas. Many people were staying at the inn,
so there was no room for Jesus and his parents. Jesus slept
in a little manger that held hay for animals.

A Prayer for the King

Father King, help me to always have room for Jesus
in my heart and life.

Princess in Action

Many people fill their lives with so much to do that they
leave Jesus out. They forget to make time to read the Bible,
pray, and go to church. Light a candle, and sing "Happy
Birthday" to Jesus. Always remember to pray and read the
Bible with your mom or dad.

December 26

Follow the Star

Royal Words

After the Wise Men had listened to [King Herod],
they went on their way. The star they had seen when
they were in the east went ahead of them. It finally
stopped over the place where the child was.
MATTHEW 2:9

Princess Thoughts

Wise men saw a special star in the sky and followed it. When they
found Jesus, they worshiped him. The wise men gave Jesus gifts of gold,
frankincense, and myrrh. Frankincense and myrrh are spices and special
oils. The gifts showed Jesus that the wise men cared about him.

A Prayer for the King

Father King, thank you for the wise men who found Jesus. Help
me to be wise.

Princess in Action

Play a game of follow the star. Let one person be the leader and
hold a paper star. Then everyone can follow the star all around the
house. The wise men followed a special star,
but God wants us to follow Jesus.

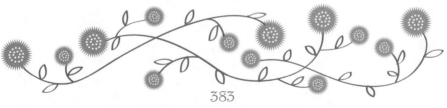

Thank-You Notes

Royal Words

I want all of you to live together in peace. Be understanding. Love one another like members of the same family. Be kind and tender. Don't be proud.

1 PETER 3:8

Princess Thoughts

Jesus came because he loves all people and wants everyone to be part of his family. He wants us to love one another like we love the people in our family. He wants us to listen to other people.

A Prayer for the King

Father King, thanks for making so many people. Help me to live in peace and show love to others.

Princess in Action

Write thank-you notes or call people to say thanks for gifts you received this Christmas.

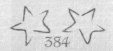

Glory to God!

Royal Words
[Jesus] has made us members of his royal family. . . .
Give him glory and power for ever and ever!
REVELATION 1:6

Princess Thoughts
When you love and obey God, you are part of his royal
family. God is the King, and you are his princess. God's royal
family sings praises to the King.

A Prayer for the King
Father God, thank you for being the King.

Princess in Action
Use pieces of garland to make a halo for your head. Every
time someone comes to visit, shout what the angels sang,
"Glory to God! Peace on earth."

December 29

Talents

Royal Words

God's gifts of grace come in many forms. Each
of you has received a gift in order to serve
others. You should use it faithfully.

1 PETER 4:10

Princess Thoughts

God gives us great gifts. That includes our talents and
abilities to help other people. God wants you to use your
gifts to help others.

A Prayer for the King

Father King, thank you for all I can do. Thank you for
giving me gifts that let me help people.

Princess in Action

Talk about your talents (what you're good at). Maybe
you are good at singing, swimming, making people smile,
or encouraging friends. Ask a parent to list your talents
on a piece of paper, or draw pictures of you doing them.
Hang the paper up as a sign that you want to use your
talents for God.

December 30

Asking God

Royal Words

Ask, and it will be given to you. Search, and you will find. Knock, and the door will be opened to you.

MATTHEW 7:7

Princess Thoughts

The devotions in this book give you many verses and thoughts about God. It's just the beginning. God invites you to keep asking him to help you. He invites you to search the Bible to learn more about him.

A Prayer for the King

Father King, help me to understand when I read the Bible. Help me to trust you to answer my prayers. Help me to remember to open my Bible and read it.

Princess in Action

Choose how you will learn more about God next year. Find a new book to read, or choose a Bible. You can even use this book again.

Do Great Things for God

Royal Words

[Jesus said,] "What I'm about to tell you is true. Anyone who has faith in me will do what I have been doing. In fact, he will do even greater things. That is because I am going to the Father."

JOHN 14:12

Princess Thoughts

Jesus loves to help you, his princess, do great things. He promises that you can do great things, even greater than what Jesus did on earth. You can ask him for help anytime.

A Prayer for the King

Lord Jesus, help me to do great things.

Princess in Action

Hooray! You finished this book. Celebrate with your family. Wear your princess crown and pretty jewels. Choose a special way to celebrate.

Scripture Index

About the Author

Karen Whiting is an author and speaker with seventeen published books, and hundreds of articles and short pieces for over four dozen publications, including *Focus on the Family* magazine and *Christian Parenting Today*. She was a contributing writer for *Focus on Your Child*, and she currently writes a quarterly article for *Enrichment Journal* for pastors and leaders of the Assemblies of God denomination and a family page for a monthly denominational newspaper. Karen has also been the community producer and host of the television series *Puppets on Parade* for Miami educational TV.

Karen has a heart for families and encourages families to connect and live more fully for God. She is a mother of five and a grandmother.

Books Just for God's Princesses

In-depth stories about women in the Bible *(for girls ages 4–8)*
978-1-4143-4811-7

A board book that introduces girls to women in the Bible *(for girls 5 and younger)*
978-1-4143-3324-3

365 devotions for God's princesses *(for girls ages 3–5)*
978-1-4143-6905-1

For more information, visit Tyndale.com/kids.

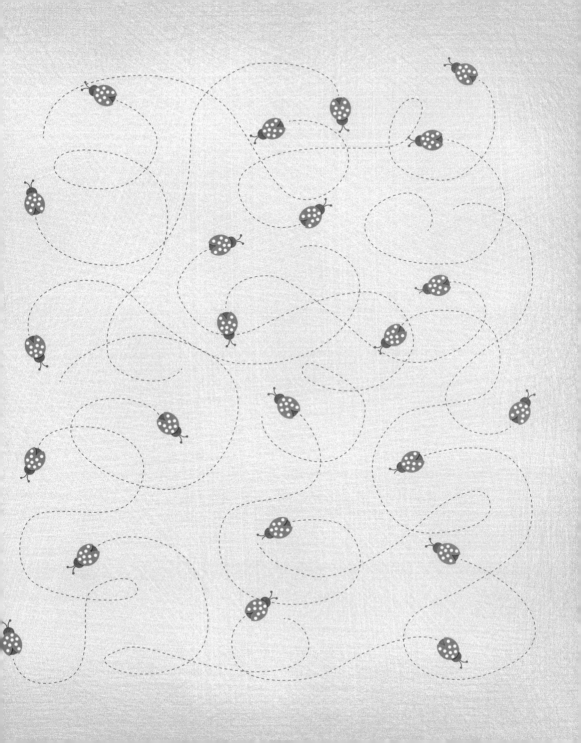